KAIt 6947
Soc

SOCIAL POLICY, CRIME AND PUNISHMENT

Jane Morgan

SOCIAL POLICY, CRIME AND PUNISHMENT

Essays in Memory of Jane Morgan

Edited by
IEUAN GWYNEDD JONES
and
GLANMOR WILLIAMS

CARDIFF
UNIVERSITY OF WALES PRESS
1994

British Library Cataloguing-in-Publication Data

A catalogue record for this book is available from the British Library.

ISBN 0–7083–1258–6

Typeset in England by The Midlands Book Typesetting Company, Loughborough
Printed in Wales by Dinefwr Press, Llandybïe

Contents

The Editors

IEUAN GWYNEDD JONES MA, D.Litt., F.R.Hist.S., is Emeritus Professor of Welsh History at University College of Wales, Aberystwyth.

GLANMOR WILLIAMS FBA, CBE, MA, D.Litt., F.R.Hist.S., is Vice President of University College of Wales, Aberystwyth.

The Contributors

SUE BALSOM completed an MA in Modern German Literature at University College of Wales, Aberystwyth, before working in teaching, journalism and careers advice. She now manages the public affairs, PR and media services company Francis Balsom Associates.

VICTOR BAILEY is Professor of Modern British History at the University of Kansas. He is the editor of *Policy and Punishment in Nineteenth-Century Britain* (Rutgers Press, 1981) and author of *Delinquency and Citizenship: Reclaiming the Young Offender, 1914–1948* (Oxford, 1987).

HENRY PHELPS BROWN MBE (Mil) FBA is Professor Emeritus of the Economics of Labour in the University of London (London School of Economics), Hon. Fellow of New College and of Wadham College, Oxford, and past president of the Royal Economic Society.

PETER CLARKE is Professor of Modern History and a Fellow of St John's College, Cambridge. His first book *Lancashire and the New Liberalism* (1971) was the source of much fruitful controversy about the fate of the Liberal Party. His most recent book, *A Question of Leadership: Gladstone to Thatcher* (1992) expands on some of the themes broached in his essay in this volume. He is a Fellow of the British Academy and writes frequently for the *Times Literary Supplement* and the *London Review of Books*.

NEIL EVANS is Tutor in History and Co-ordinator of the Centre for Welsh Studies at Coleg Harlech and Honorary Lecturer in the School of History and Welsh History, University College of North Wales, Bangor. He has published widely on the history of Wales and the British Isles and is writing a book, *Darker Cardiff: the Underside of the City, 1840–1960*.

ELAINE GENDERS is a lecturer in Laws (criminal justice and criminal law) at University College London. She was a Research Fellow at the Centre for Criminological Research, Oxford, from 1980 until 1990. She is joint author, with Elaine Player, of *Race Relations in Prisons* (OUP, 1989) and *A Therapeutic Prison: A Study of Grendon* (forthcoming, OUP).

DICK HOBBS is a lecturer in the Department of Sociology and Social Policy at the University of Durham. His research interests are police culture, working-class culture and professional and organized crime.

ROGER HOOD is a Fellow of All Souls College, University Reader in Criminology and Director of the Centre for Criminological Research at Oxford. He is a Fellow of the British Academy and a past president of the British Society of Criminology. He is co-author with Sir Leon Radzinowicz of *The Emergence of Penal Policy* (Vol. 5 of *A History of English Criminal Law*, Stevens, 1986) and his most recent books are *The Death Penalty: A World-Wide Perspective* (OUP, 1989) and *Race and Sentencing* (OUP, 1992).

DAVID J. V. JONES is Professor of History at the University College of Swansea and a Fellow of the Royal Historical Society. His main interest is the history of working people, and their politics, protests and illegal activities. He is the author of seven books on modern English and Welsh social history, including *Crime, Policy and Protest in Nineteenth-Century Britain* (Routledge 1984), *Rebecca's Children* (OUP, 1989) and *Crime in Nineteenth-Century Wales* (University of Wales Press, 1992).

ROD MORGAN is Professor of Criminal Justice and Dean of Law at the University of Bristol. He is author of many books and articles on criminal justice and, most recently, co-editor of *The Oxford Handbook of Criminology* (OUP, 1994). He is an expert consultant to the Council of Europe and Amnesty International.

HELEN MUIR is a former *Sunday Times* journalist. She writes children's books and novels. Her latest novel, *Consequences* will be published in June 1994 (Simon and Schuster).

JILL PEAY is a lecturer in the Department of Law at Brunel University and a practising barrister. From 1980 to 1988 she was a Research Fellow at the Centre for Criminological Research, Oxford. Her research interests include mental health law and the prosecution process. She is the author of *Tribunals on Trial: A Study of Decision-making under the Mental Health Act 1983* (Clarendon Press, 1989).

ELAINE PLAYER is a lecturer in the Law School, King's College, London. She is the co-author (with Elaine Genders) of *Race Relations in Prisons* (OUP, 1989) and a forthcoming study of Grendon prison, *A Therapeutic Prison* (OUP).

JOHN WILLIAMS is a senior lecturer in Law and Dean of the Faculty of Economics and Social Studies at the University College of Wales, Aberystwyth. He has published a number of books and articles on the law relating to social services and mental health. Most recently he has edited a collection of essays with Christopher Harding, *Legal Provision in Rural Areas* (University of Wales Press, 1994).

'J. P. WOODSTOCK': this piece was submitted on behalf of the Woodstock Bench by Mrs Diana Peverel-Cooper, Chairman.

LUCIA ZEDNER is Lecturer in Law and Assistant Director of the Mannheim Centre for Criminology and Criminal Justice at the London School of Economics. Her publications include *Women, Crime, and Custody in Victorian England* (1991); with Jane Morgan, *Child Victims: Crime, Impact, and Criminal Justice* (1992); with L. H. Leigh, Royal Commission on Criminal Justice Research Study No. 1 (1992).

Foreword

The tragic circumstances of the death in August 1992 of Dr Jane Morgan, wife of the Principal, Professor Kenneth Morgan, were deeply distressing to everyone associated with the College. Although she and her husband and children had been in Aberystwyth for only just over three years, Jane, a young, vital, energetic, handsome woman had endeared herself to us all. A distinguished former student of the College, she had taken to the role of Principal's wife and helpmate with consummate ease and grace. Her loss at the tragically early age of forty-two was a crushing blow to everybody.

At her funeral service on 13 August the tribute paid to Jane by her friend and former teacher, Professor Ieuan Gwynedd Jones, was intensely moving; so touching that many of us felt that it ought to be published in order that it might reach all those who knew and loved Jane but were not able to be at her funeral. From that suggestion sprang the idea that it might be fitting to add to Professor Jones's tribute a collection of papers on subjects on which she had worked in recent years and had intended to work in the future, together with a number of reminiscences of her. I was very pleased to pledge the whole-hearted support of the College for such a venture. I should like to thank, warmly and sincerely, those of Jane's friends and colleagues who have so readily agreed to contribute to the volume and Professors Ieuan Gwynedd Jones and Glanmor Williams for acting as its editors. This book, and the decision to name the student village at Aberystwyth after Jane, will provide a lasting memorial to her; a permanent focus for those chords of memory of one who had already achieved so much and would certainly have had a great deal more to give.

Sir Melvyn Rosser
President of the University of Wales, Aberystwyth

Editors' Introduction

Although Jane graduated in history and, in the course of her postgraduate work and later, gave ample evidence of her ability in the field of recent history, she also performed the notable feat of turning herself into a first-rate criminologist, with a special concern for the treatment of offenders. We therefore thought it proper that, in asking some of her friends to write for this memorial volume to her, we should invite essays from historians and from other scholars with a particular interest in those aspects of criminology with which Jane had been profoundly concerned in recent years. The first three deal with subjects drawn from contemporary history, while the remaining five discuss criminological and legal issues of great contemporary relevance and even controversy. Additionally, we considered it to be appropriate to include a number of short pieces which incorporated their authors' recollections of some facets of Jane's many-sided activities and interests. It was not possible to include contributions from all her friends who would have wished to be associated with the book, but we hope that we have provided a representative cross-section of the qualities and pursuits that characterized this remarkably attractive and versatile personality.

In the process of editing this volume we have incurred many debts which we should like gratefully to acknowledge. We wish to thank Sir Melvyn Rosser, President of the College, for all his staunch support throughout; Professor Kenneth Morgan, Principal, for an immense amount of help and co-operation at a particularly difficult time in his life; and Mr Daniel Gruffydd Jones, Registrar, and his secretary, Ms Pat Jones, for so readily putting the resources of their office at our disposal. We should also like especially to thank the authors of the essays and the reminiscences for their splendid co-operation. They not only unhesitatingly agreed to contribute to the volume but all of them also completed their task with exemplary punctuality. We are further indebted to Ms Susan Jenkins and Ms Liz Powell of the University of Wales Press for their help and interest in seeing the book through the press. We hope that our combined efforts will have resulted in a memorial worthy of one who was held in such deep admiration and affection by us all.

IEUAN GWYNEDD JONES   GLANMOR WILLIAMS

Jane Morgan (1949–1992)

Jane was born Jane Keeler in Harrogate on 21 October 1949. She remained deeply attached to the Yorkshire spa town thereafter. Her father was German and her mother British. Her ancestry, in fact, was a mixture of German, Russian, Scottish and Welsh, which contributed to her striking physical appearance. A distinguished politician once referred perceptively to her 'hybrid vivacity'.

Her childhood was in some ways a hard one. Her father was killed in a car crash before she was born and she thus grew up in a one-parent family. At the age of four, she moved with her mother to Wrexham, her grandmother's home. Here she went to Acton Park School and then to Grove Park School for Girls. Despite the difficulties of her upbringing, Jane grew up a happy, lively and attractive girl, with a particular love of ponies and much skill in games and gymnastics. At Grove Park she developed an intense love for history, encouraged by private visitations to the library of Erddig at the invitation of the lovable eccentric, Philip Yorke, before that great house was acquired by the National Trust. She gained very strong A levels in history, English and religious studies, and in 1968 began her long association with the University College of Wales, Aberystwyth, as a student reading history. She would delight to mention how she picked out Aberystwyth from a teenage magazine, *Honey*, which focused on the relative preponderance of men students at the 'College by the Sea'.

She loved the student life at Aberystwyth, above all, the two years in Alexandra Hall, overlooking Cardigan Bay. She represented Aber at netball, she participated in the 'rag', she even won a student beauty competition! But, always, she was deeply serious about her historical studies and an indefatigable worker in the college and National libraries. In 1971 she obtained a fine degree which won her two prizes for history. More important, she also gained a postgraduate studentship which enabled her to start on a further MA degree, mainly in nineteenth-century Welsh history under the supervision of Professor Ieuan Gwynedd Jones. This caused her to abandon her previous wish for a career in social work, although she retained a strong interest in practical social and welfare issues throughout her life. This also influenced her bent for social history, shown in her well-constructed MA thesis on the 1868 general election in Denbighshire, itself as much a study of social structure as of party politics.

In 1972 she was awarded a position as a researcher to the Board of Celtic Studies, working on a schedule of the parliamentary papers relating to Wales from 1868 onwards. This work took her to the British Library in London and to a flat in Ealing. By this time, too, she had met Kenneth Morgan, a Fellow in Modern History and Politics at The Queen's College, Oxford. The courtship began in the newspaper room of the National Library of Wales; he proposed in a café opposite the British Museum. They married in Aberystwyth on 4 January 1973. They settled down in a succession of villages to the north-west of Oxford; Eynsham briefly, then East End near to a Roman villa, and finally in 1976 in Long Hanborough, Jane's home until she died. They had two children, David, born in July 1974, and Katherine, born in September 1977.

Jane was a warm and devoted wife and mother, deeply happy in her family life. She was also gregarious and a vivacious hostess who loved entertaining friends and undergraduates. The family highlights included holidays, initially in various parts of rural France, then from 1984 in Italy, particularly Tuscany and Umbria which Jane especially loved. She also found time for other activities including riding and the Church at North Leigh. But Jane's absorption with history soon found its outlet, too. With the help of a local child-minder she began an external Ph.D. at the University of Leicester, under the effective supervision of her husband, on the political career of Christopher, Viscount Addison, a close associate of Lloyd George who made the transition from Liberalism to Labour. Wary meetings with Addison's aged widow in High Wycombe were a feature of

Jane's research, although the basis was a careful study of the massive Addison Papers in the Bodleian. Despite the demands of two young children, she gained her doctorate in 1979, with Dr (now Professor) Peter Clarke as external examiner. The revised thesis was published, under the joint authorship of husband and wife, by Oxford University Press in 1980 under the title *Portrait of a Progressive*. It received warm praise in the press from Stephen Koss, John Grigg and Max Beloff amongst others.

Jane's academic interests were now beginning to move away from history. Indeed, the aspect of Addison's career which particularly fascinated her was his pioneer work as first Minister of Health. She worked briefly as assistant to the eminent Oxford labour historian, Sir Henry Phelps Brown, in 1979 on a major volume published in 1983 under the title *The Origins of Trade Union Power*. But a major turning point came later that year when she was appointed research officer to work with Dr (now Professor) Victor Bailey on a Home Office project on British penal policy between 1919 and 1939, based in Worcester College, Oxford. For the next two years, she was engrossed in the work at the Public Record Office that led ultimately to the publication of Dr Bailey's *Delinquency and Citizenship* (OUP, 1987). This stimulated a growing absorption with the law and criminology which dominated her work thereafter. She also became research officer at the Centre for Criminological Research in north Oxford; later she became a research fellow and then research associate. She became a popular and enthusiastic participant in the seminars and social life of the Centre, and made close friends there.

In 1982 she won a 'Thank Offering to Britain' research fellowship from the British Academy, being interviewed by (and charming) such eminences as Isaiah Berlin, Herbert Hart and Owen Chadwick in the process. She now began work on a pioneering study of the role of the police in labour disputes in England and Wales between 1900 and 1939. This bridged her growing interest in the police and public order with her long-standing concern with modern British history. Her work entailed minute research into the public records in Kew and the Home Office itself, along with a vast array of local police records, especially in south Wales. It demanded from Jane considerable stamina as well as clarity of thought. But the results were impressive and were shown in a widely acclaimed book published by Oxford University Press in 1987 – *Conflict and Order*. Central themes of the book were its account of growing Home Office influence over the provincial police; the role of the police in the government's anti-strike apparatus after 1918; the widespread use of the armed forces in labour disputes; and the decline in police accountability. Operational aspects included the police response to picketing and to the unemployed marches of the inter-war years. In this book, Jane's sympathies with the underdog as well as her academic skills were fully engaged. The events of the national miners' strike in 1984–5 gave her findings contemporary relevance. The reception was uniformly enthusiastic, from Michael Foot in the *Guardian* to academic reviewers in *History*, the *English Historical Review*, the *American Historical Review* and *Albion*.

Jane then became involved in a number of smaller projects. She assisted Sir Alec Cairncross on his study of British economic policy, 1945–52, *Years of Recovery* (1985). She worked for a time with Dr Tony Harrison of Policy Journals on Crime UK, supported by the Nuffield Foundation, investigating the scale of resources that the public and private sectors were putting into crime prevention and law enforcement, and dealing with the consequences of crime. She also worked for the Runnymede Trust on London Court records dealing with the highly contentious theme of race and sentencing, which made a lasting impression on her.

But the most important project of all came in 1987 when she was appointed to work, initially with Joyce Plotnikoff, later with Dr Lucia Zedner, on a project – funded by the Home Office – on 'Children as Victims of Crime: Impact, Needs, and Responses'. This three-year study examined the effects of crime on children, focusing especially on Oxford and Bedfordshire. It was also conducted in liaison with the National Association of Victim Support to assess the work and effectiveness of the various social and legal agencies, and especially of Victim Support schemes. This major project, and the book that resulted from it, *Child Victims*, absorbed much of Jane's intellectual energies until just before her death.

Life in Oxford in the 1980s was for Jane particularly full and pleasant. The children were growing up happily. Life in Queen's and Oxford generally was sociable and varied. She had dining rights at Worcester, St Hilda's and later Brasenose. There were endless rides or walks in the Oxfordshire countryside, alternating with visits to London, perhaps to publishers' or newspaper literary parties, perhaps to meet friends like Alan and Eva Taylor in Twisden Road, or Michael and Jill Foot in Hampstead (though never a politician, Jane had strong, and growing, radical and social sympathies). In Oxfordshire, Jane and the children found time for much riding, while holidays saw the family make their way to Aberystwyth or Wrexham to see the mothers. When Kenneth was offered the principalship of the University College of Wales, Aberystwyth, at the beginning of 1988, it was a difficult decision as to whether to face so great a personal upheaval. In fact, Jane's own happy memories of Aberystwyth and a general family attachment to friends in the University of Wales left the outcome in little doubt. From April 1989 Jane was resident in Aberystwyth.

Here she soon blossomed. She played her full part as Principal's wife, as a gracious and stylish hostess at Plas Penglais. But she was always active and creative in her own right. She became an honorary lecturer in the Aberystwyth Law Department, and showed herself to be an effective lecturer and tutor on criminological and penal themes. She also taught in the Department of Social Theory in Bangor in 1990–91 and proved to be equally effective there. Since 1986 she had been a Justice of the Peace, and a very successful one, on the Woodstock bench in Oxfordshire, and she continued her service there after moving to Aberystwyth. This meant long evening drives for Jane every other Monday from Bangor to Long Hanborough; but she always emerged apparently undiminished in energy, always radiant and irrepressible.

She was becoming well known in the criminological world, as British Society of Criminology *Newsletter* editor and a frequent and confident participant in the British Criminology Conference and similar gatherings. Despite what appeared to Jane and Kenneth to be excessive Home Office caution, which gave Jane needless worry, she successfully completed her report on child victims in early 1990, with Lucia Zedner (now of the London School of Economics), an academic colleague who also became a very close personal friend. A separate report was produced for the National Association of Victim Support, evaluating the Association's schemes in Bedfordshire. A central feature of the research were the interviews Jane conducted with children and their parents in Oxford and Bedfordshire, often about less serious offences but sometimes with victims of cruel assault or racial crimes. Always Jane was an effective questioner and sympathetic listener. On scores of occasions there were lengthy evening car journeys in all weathers from Long Hanborough to Bedford, Luton, Leighton Buzzard or elsewhere. Always Jane emerged indefatigable.

In March 1992 *Child Victims*, written with Lucia Zedner, was published by Oxford University Press. This book variously analyses the nature of crimes against children, surveys the agencies dealing with children and their families, examines the role of the police and the way in which children were handled by the criminal justice system, and makes suggestions about public policy. The reception suggested that an important area of criminological inquiry had been pioneered, and the book's publication attracted much media attention. Jane herself made several very effective presentations of the book's findings on the radio and in interviews with national newspapers. Her successful live interview with Brian Redhead on the 'Today' programme on Radio Four showed that she was wholly comfortable with this largely unfamiliar medium. Meanwhile, she was moving on to other areas of social research with colleagues in Aberystwyth. With John Williams, she produced a valuable study of family health services for the Dyfed Family Health Service Authority; she was also developing plans for a regional crime survey with

Laurence Koffman, and a survey on women and community care with Sue Charles. She also attended the Women's Studies Group. Her work on child victims, therefore, only spurred her on to wider areas of inquiry.

In the early summer of 1992, Jane's life seemed very full and totally happy. Life with Kenneth at Aberystwyth was wholly enjoyable. She had important duties as a magistrate, and as founder of the Dyfed Victim Support scheme, launched at Carmarthen on a brilliantly sunny day in May. She was chairman-elect of the music club (she was always passionately musical with a devotion to opera). A major new activity was membership of the Welsh Arts Council in 1991, on which she was soon taking a lively part as the strategic plan for the nineties was being formulated. In 1992 also came the centenary of the Aberystwyth Old Students' Association with Jane as an energetic vice-president. There was also fascinating travel to India (including the Taj Mahal) in January 1991 for the Commonwealth vice-chancellors' conference, and a trip to Malaysia in January 1992, when Jane's lectures on her research on children to social workers in Kuala Terengganu and to lawyers in Kuala Lumpur were a memorable highlight. She came back arrayed in Malaysian batik dresses in the bright colours she loved. The children's half-term in the last week of May, a time of glorious sunshine in Aberystwyth, was idyllic.

Then on 31 May she complained of pains in her stomach; they spread to her back. On 12 June she attended an Old Students' reception at the House of Lords, looking as well as ever, but now in some pain. On 26 June, cancer of the liver, a very rare viral type, was diagnosed. Chemotherapy could not save her; the fact that she had enjoyed excellent health throughout her life made her a more vulnerable target for the disease. She tried to finish a collaborative article with a Dutch colleague but could not do so. She died in Aberystwyth on 7 August at the age of forty-two. A week later, she was buried in Church Hanborough, near to the porch of the thirteenth-century parish church. There were almost a thousand letters of sympathy. That

November, the University Council at Aberystwyth decided that the thousand-strong student village at Penglais, across the road from the campus where she was a student, would bear her name. There, in her books and articles, and in memories of her unique personality, Jane will live on for ever.

Jane Morgan: A Tribute

IEUAN GWYNEDD JONES

(Memorial Service, 13 August 1992, Aberystwyth)

We who are gathered in this ancient and lovely church to pay our last respects to Jane Morgan, wife and mother, historian, colleague, and friend, have much in common. We share the same desire, and we all feel the same need for comfort. We all knew Jane Morgan with more or less intimacy. Some of you were her contemporaries as undergraduates or were her tutors when she came to Aberystwyth from Wrexham to read history. That was a mere twenty-three years ago. Almost all of us will have been recipients of her bounty in Plas Penglais and experienced the natural grace and warmth of her welcome there. Others will have been taught by her in the law department or heard her speaking to the voluntary societies, social and cultural, in which she was so active. The desire we share is to pay tribute to her memory, and to mourn her loss with the loved ones who are left behind. To Kenneth and the children, David and Katherine, and to her mother, Mrs Keeler, we extend our profoundest and most sincere sympathy.

When I look back over the twenty years and more that I have known Jane I am struck by the symmetries that are revealed. There are the obvious geographical ones: her education in Aberystwyth and her return after eighteen years as the wife of the Principal, her academic life ending where it began. But at a profounder level I can detect in her final published research and writings the fulfilment of her early ideals, the coming to fruition of her deepest, most human interests. Social history was her forte: her splendid Master's dissertation was on the election of 1868 in Denbighshire, but it was the social movements underlying the events of that year that absorbed her attention, especially the political aspirations of the working class about which we knew so little and which conventional political historians tended to ignore. After graduating MA she was appointed as a researcher for the Board of Celtic Studies, and it was during this time that, to the great joy of those who knew them both, she met and married Kenneth Morgan, who was at that time Fellow in Modern History at The Queen's College, Oxford. Her next project, for which she gained her doctorate from Leicester University, was on the political career of one of the century's most important, though neglected, social reformers, Christopher, Viscount Addison. You will recall that a version of this important study, written in collaboration with her husband, was published by Oxford University Press in 1988. Even more important, I think, was the work she did on the police and labour disputes in Britain. This was published under the title *Conflict and Order* by OUP in 1987, just a few years after the traumatic events of the miners' strike of 1984. This book is a superb contribution to social history, especially to the social history of south Wales, using sources to which no historian had had access before. Her latest and, alas, final research was on penal policy. This cut into the deepest levels of our society and showed – indeed, warned us – that child abuse is part of a much wider culture of neglect and cruelty, and almost invariably the product of inequality and social deprivation. It would be foolish to claim too much, but I think that it was here in Aber that this interest in the deeper levels of society was first aroused and articulated.

That was a kind of progression. But there is another. It is that Jane's work after leaving Aber had an intensely and increasingly practical purpose. She was no desiccated scholar; far from it. A fine idealism drove her in the direction of social reform. Understand how society works, how it is structured, in order to improve it was her philosophy, as it has always been the philosophy of social reformers. *Child Victims*, which she wrote in collaboration with Dr Lucia Zedner, was reviewed in *The Magistrate* in the very week that her cruel disease was diagnosed. The closing sentence of the review is an exhortation to every magistrate and judge to study the book with the greatest care and attention. She saw the review and it must have pleased her. It was evidence that she was being taken seriously.

Of course, Jane was a very serious person with regard to her work. She fretted at the endless tergiversations of civil servants and government departments. She took infinite pains with her research and worked incredibly hard, never sparing herself. Even as an undergraduate she would work whole days in the National Library without even a tea break. When she was doing full-time research this was the normal pattern of her days. But she was never a solemn person; on the contrary she was a happy, vivacious, gregarious, lively young woman, quick to respond in the cut and thrust of conversation, full of wit and humour. Who can forget her lovely smile, her welcoming embrace, her ability to put you at your ease and at the centre of things? But she loved silences too, the silence of the early morning before the town is awake, the solitary rides along the bridle-paths above Penglais. Above all, she loved the silences of libraries, silences made eloquent by the rustle of pages turned, of books raised and put down, those creative silences when ideas form in the mind and are written down. And now, at the end, at these her obsequies, I find it difficult to believe that a life so rich, so full, so life-enhancing for others, so useful has been so suddenly removed from among us.

What consolation is there for Ken, and David and Katherine and Jessica? And for us who mourn with them? For those of us who believe, there are the truths and certainties that have been embodied in the liturgy of which we are now, at this very moment, a part. For all, whether we believe, or strive to believe, or cannot believe, there are the peace and symbolism of this wonderful building where generation upon generation have come to bid a last farewell to their loved ones. The flowers with which the College Women's Club have so carefully and tastefully decorated the church will soon fade: 'gwywa y gwelltyn, syrth y blodeuyn' (the grass withereth, the flower fadeth): but the memory of Jane will not quickly fade in the hearts and minds of those who so lovingly arranged them and brought them here. That is a real consolation, as is the undoubted fact that Jane's books will stand the test of time and be of service to future generations. It might be said of her (to use the words of a contemporary of her favourite poet, Donne), that these were the trophies she erected 'Against the dark and Time's consuming Rage'. And always there are the friends to whom Ken and his family can turn for consolation and support.

Fe gyfrannodd hon yn helaeth i'n dealltwriaeth ni fel Cymry o'n gorffennol, yn enwedig am y gymdeithas oedd yn bodoli yn Oes Fictoria ac o'r gymdeithas sydd ohoni heddiw. Yr oedd yn gymeriad hoffus a thirion ac yr oedd yn caru'r gwirionedd. Yr oedd yn caru ein cenedl ni. Heddwch i'w llwch.

I

SOCIAL POLICY, CRIME AND PUNISHMENT

1

Crime in the South Wales Police District, 1969–1989

DAVID J. V. JONES

This chapter is a small contribution to the history of crime and policing in the twentieth century. The region and the dates are carefully chosen. The south Wales police district, with a population of one and a quarter million people, was, and remains, the largest in Wales and the only one of a truly metropolitan character. The year 1969 was the first year of the amalgamated South Wales Constabulary, which included the once-independent police districts of Cardiff, Swansea, and Merthyr Tydfil, as well as the old county of Glamorgan; and twenty years later, on its anniversary, the latest Chief Constable, W. R. Lawrence, took office against a background of public anxiety about crime, and political pressures for change. The year 1989 was a time for evaluating the legacy of the past, and considering radical plans for the future.

At first glance, the story of crime and policing in the twenty years after amalgamation was one of disappointment. Although Cardiff objected strongly to aspects of the merger of the police forces, there was considerable optimism in 1969, springing partly from a belief in the virtues of integrated policing and panda-car patrols. The Chief Constable, Melbourne Thomas, hoped that once the combined force had settled down, there would be a new 'momentum in the fields of prevention and detection'. Thirteen years later, one of his successors, David East, believed that the battle was at last 'swinging against the criminals'. However, by the time of his departure at the end of 1988, the overwhelming impression, from the media, interviews, surveys and statistics, was that things had got worse, and some of the early enthusiasm for crime prevention and community policing had begun to evaporate.

When asked in the 1980s to describe the experience of crime, people in south Wales often referred to a set of familiar and photographic images. These mental pictures were of beaten pensioners, drunken and drugged youngsters, angry strikers and demonstrators, burgled premises, fire-ravaged schools, and stolen cars. Some of these images had an impact out of all proportion to the incidence of the delinquency which they illustrated. Fear, as much as experience, has always been important in the story of crime, and in the way it has been recorded and treated.

Psychological studies have shown that over recent decades many elderly people and single women have become alarmed about aspects of modern living, and the temptation has been to play upon such anxieties. Early in 1982 Chief Constable John Woodcock warned of the dangers of exaggerating the problem of crime, but the media concentration on the worst figures and cases only increased the sense of insecurity. In 1986 there was a predictably angry reaction to the announcement that one indictable crime was committed every five minutes in the south Wales police district, and three years later, after dense newspaper and TV coverage, places like the Ely council estate in Cardiff and the Kingsway entertainment zone in Swansea seemed for a while to be synonymous with crime and violence. Not surprisingly, when asked for their views at the end of our period, the ordinary man or woman in the street declared that 'times have never been worse'.

It is difficult to establish the validity of popular notions regarding the level of delinquency. They do not always match the historical perspective, policing experience and official statistics. We know, from the British Crime Surveys, that the reporting of crime is by no means comprehensive, its completeness varying greatly from one type of offence and community to another. Amongst the most poorly reported of crimes are criminal damage, sexual offences and family violence. One estimate, based on a small sample in the British Crime Survey of 1983, suggests that the Welsh, even more than the English, are much more likely to report burglaries and thefts from houses than assaults. Even so, about four offences in five remain unreported.

Rural inhabitants within south Wales, like those elsewhere, have historically been more reluctant to report crimes than townsfolk, whilst across urban and industrial districts there have also been significant differences, depending in part on the sociology and geography of individual neighbourhoods. Thus, for example, close-knit mining communities, like Troedyrhiw, with its long memories of industrial disputes, have been slow to use the police, whilst Bishopston in Gower has not. Even so, during the years 1969–89 the general trend throughout south Wales was a greater willingness to report offences to the authorities. This was a result of, amongst other things, better communications, the requirements of insurance policies, and the influence of community policing, watch schemes and other attempts to increase an interest in the problem of crime. Such has been the reaction that patrolling policemen in the 1980s spent much, if not most, of their time dealing with calls from the public, and in the middle of the decade the force was obliged to introduce a 'graded response' system.

The historian, more than the criminologist or sociologist, has to rely heavily on the evidence provided by these policemen. The limitations of the official criminal statistics are well known. They have never been a complete record of known offences, and they contain artificial elements. From time to time, for example, the Home Office, chief constables, and other agencies gave certain crimes a high profile, and the subsequent returns must be seen in this light. Similarly, new legislation like the Criminal Damage Act (1971) and the Public Order Act (1986) distorted the view of the unfolding criminal scene. So did the changes in the classification and cataloguing of offences, most notably in 1969, 1979 and 1988.

The published police statistics indicated that the south Wales district had a deserved reputation for being one of the most criminal areas in Britain. In 1989 only eight police forces returned worse figures. In that year the number of recorded indictable offences was 112,255, and another 58,645 people were cautioned and prosecuted for non-indictable offences (other than motoring), a combined total which, when set against the population, represented a doubling of the rate of twenty years before. The rate of serious crimes – which is the starting-point of our enquiry – rose even faster, with the steepest climb being in the years 1979–86, the period of the miners' strike, high levels of unemployment, angry complaints from the most deprived areas of south Wales, and protests over the slow-down in police recruitment.

In a Welsh context the rate of recorded indictable crime in this district was almost two and a half times worse in 1989 than that of Dyfed–Powys. Within the district, too, there were marked differences; thus, South Glamorgan in 1989 had a crime rate twice as bad as that of Mid Glamorgan, and 50 per cent worse than that of West Glamorgan. Of the eight divisions within the police district, Cardiff Central in 1989 had over 24,000 reported indictable offences for every 100,000 of its population, whilst next on the list, Cardiff Greater and Swansea, had over 9,000; though significantly they also had less than half the number of policemen per head of population. Four years before, when Swansea had two police divisions, Swansea Central had over 11,000 reported offences per 100,000 inhabitants, and Swansea West (including Gower) was the best in the south Wales district, with just over 4,000. Although there were a few exceptions, the pattern established before the industrial revolution persists; the more urbanized the area, the more crime is reported.

Within that general pattern there were, of course, important variations. The centres of Cardiff, Swansea, Merthyr, and Pontypridd, had high rates of crime, especially of shop-lifting, the stealing of motor vehicles and public disorder, but there were other neighbourhoods where the police were almost as busy. These included residential localities like Roath Park, which attracted burglars; places of mixed housing and industrial premises, such as Fforestfach in Swansea; and socially deprived communities dominated by large council estates. Not all council estates had high crime rates, but at Gurnos and Penrhys, for example, there was a notoriously large number of complaints, incidents and offences. Sometimes, as at Bonymaen and Winchwen in Swansea, local criminals often travelled some distance before committing their offences, whilst the inhabitants of Canton or Peterston-super-Ely regarded themselves as the victims of 'outsiders'.

The places with the lowest crime rates were usually villages, settled industrial communities like Blaenrhondda, and fairly isolated suburbs. By 1989 no one was unaware of the rising crime figures, but the experience of people living in, for instance, the centre of Mountain Ash or a short distance away in Miskin was very different. To a degree, the scale and character of delinquency in these places reflected the history of the community; areas of rapid growth were often characterized by disorder and theft, whilst areas of decline became accustomed to offences associated with drink, depression and boredom.

The published information on the seasonality and cost of crime is of limited value. A sample of 472,251 crimes committed against the person and property between 1981 and 1989 indicated that the reports of these offences were at their height during March. The spring, and the start of the winter seasons, were the most criminal periods, with June–September usually comparatively quiet. Burglaries had a rather different seasonality, the highest figures being in the first three months of the year, whilst assaults, and sometimes public disorder and sexual offences, peaked in the four hottest months, notably during the hours between 8 p.m. and 4 a.m.

The cost of these crimes can never be properly assessed. Some radical observers have argued that, when set in the wider context of national income and losses, the problem of crime has been exaggerated, perhaps deliberately so. Certainly, deaths from criminal activities were rare, though to the average of thirteen homicides a year in the south Wales police district must be added a hundred killed by reckless or careless driving and perhaps a quarter or half that total who died after illegally obtaining drugs. In addition, a considerable number of people were injured during violent assaults, and several hundred of these, including many policemen, lodged claims every year with the Criminal Injuries Compensation Board. Finally, Victim Support groups, established across south Wales in the late 1980s, helped even larger numbers of people who had suffered from serious attacks and burglaries.

The cost of property crime is only slightly easier to estimate. The police have been obliged, since the mid-nineteenth century, to provide information each year on the value of stolen property. By 1980 the figure in the south Wales district had risen to £13,552,360, and nine years later it had reached over £53,483,221, or £620 per crime. The stealing of motor vehicles, thefts from cars, and burglaries were largely responsible for this average figure, for over 40 per cent of offences were costed at below £100. The frequent discovery of stolen vehicles also distorted the recovery rate; in 1989 some 42.5 per cent of the value of stolen property was recovered, but the rate for most thefts, including burglaries, was much worse than this.

The crimes recorded in the south Wales police district in recent decades were rather different in character from those recorded prior to the Second World War. In particular, offences against the person formed a larger part of the police statistics of indictable crime. There was a rapid increase, almost five-fold, in the rate of recorded acts of violence during the years 1969–89. Even so, contrary to impressions sometimes given in the media, this rate was usually well below that of Gwent, and, occasionally, that of north Wales. If one avoided the late-night revels in the centres of Cardiff, Swansea, Barry, Merthyr Tydfil and a few other places, the chances of men and women being attacked outside the home were remarkably small.

Homicides numbered only 13 per year during our period. The context and nature of these violent deaths had changed very little from earlier times. Over 60 per cent of homicides were committed by persons related or known to the victims. Classic victims were three elderly wives of Cardiff, Nelson and Cwmavon, killed by their husbands in 1982, quarrelsome lovers, and young people caught up in a brawl. Infanticide, by contrast, had become extremely rare in the district, at least so far as can be ascertained.

As in pre-war years, most publicity was given to the least common types of killings, like the shooting of a car driver during a robbery at Penllergaer in 1978, and the murders in the 1980s of a Swansea sex-shop manageress and the Cardiff prostitute Lynette White. Other violence against the person also received rather unbalanced media attention. Of the few kidnapping and torture cases perhaps the most serious was that in 1979 of the Spaniard, recently released from prison, who seized members of his wife's family and set fire to the room in which he had secured them.

Armed robbery occasioned injuries to taxi-drivers, post-mistresses, garage attendants and pensioners, but less perhaps than the newspapers suggested and the elderly imagined. The anxiety of the old was reinforced by the manner in which evidence on serious assaults was presented. Of the average of more than 2,000 woundings recorded annually in the years 1969–89, a minority were committed by the young on the elderly, but these were the ones commonly selected in speeches and reports to illustrate the moral decline of modern society.

On sexual attacks, the statistical evidence is notoriously unreliable. The problem is highlighted by the fact that over the years 1969–89 south Wales had, in contrast to the situation of a century before, the lowest rate (usually below 40 per 100,000) of sexual offences recorded in the Welsh police districts, and one that generally fell until the very end of the period. Contemporaries claimed that the emergence of the feminist movement, greater publicity and more sensitive policing had improved the reporting of rape, but the number of cases that came to light, like the recorded incidence of buggery, was still small. Again, it was the sensational stories which made the headlines, such as the horrific attack by a gang of Hell's Angels on a housewife in 1979, and the case of the man and his companion imprisoned in 1984 for offering lifts to women, and then raping them. Less was heard, at least outside confidential files, of the indecent assaults on children by relatives, minders and friends.

There was some truth in the contemporary view that most of the violence in modern society was the responsibility of the young. The great majority of people apprehended for such behaviour were in their teens and early twenties, and many of their assaults were on one another, and, less commonly, on older people and the police. The late 1980s witnessed a small explosion of street violence by the youths of the largest towns of the district, centred on the public house, night club and dance hall. In 1989 gangs from Baglan and Briton Ferry, and Whitchurch and Cathays, fought each other in bloody conflict, whilst elsewhere there was the regular weekend problem of hundreds of young people, looking for drink, entertainment and excitement. At times, the excitement took the form of criminal damage, and frequently there were running battles with the police.

The latter were more carefully chronicled than other assaults; they indicate that in the 1980s injuries to the police (and their cars) in Cardiff and Swansea, and in the Cynon and upper Afan Valleys, had reached levels possibly unknown since the 1870s. Days lost, and injuries sustained, were estimated in 1986 to be approximately 20 per cent above the totals of 1979, and in 1989 the number of attacks on officers stood at a peak of 759. A survey by Lesley Noaks and other members of the University College of Cardiff indicates that certain valley communities were especially dangerous for the police, but everywhere clashes at the time of arrest were common, and damage was inflicted on numerous police cars and, more rarely, on police stations.

Family violence has always received less attention than the riot, though it was both a time-consuming and awkward problem for the authorities. In 1978 a total of 6,534 domestic disputes were recorded by the police, with especially high figures in the sub-divisions of Sketty, Morriston, Ely and Merthyr. Eleven years later, in the Bridgend police division, with a population of 134,400, officers in 1989 were called to almost 2,500 domestic disputes, some of which began or ended in violence. Over the years a combination of housing and employment problems has probably increased tensions within the home, whilst the establishment of shelters for battered wives, and the greater interest shown in child abuse, have brought more cases of family conflict to light. The extent of child cruelty and physical abuse remains especially difficult to estimate, not least before the introduction of three specialist police units in 1991, which dealt with 2,467 incidents.

During the years 1969–89 a more rigorous approach was adopted towards public order, and sanctioned by new industrial relations legislation and by statutes such as the Public Order Act of 1986. The period witnessed several public order crises, one of the most persistent being the behaviour of football crowds. Sections of Newport, Swansea, and especially Cardiff supporters were responsible for acts of vandalism and violence that reached a climax in 1987. A small number of fans were killed or maimed, and several hundred hooligans arrested each year, that is, until the recent improvement in crowd behaviour, and the joint initiatives of the clubs and the police.

Unlike some districts of Britain, protest demonstrations and racial hatred were contained in the south Wales district. There were many marches and public gatherings over cuts in health financing, social and educational provisions during the 1980s, as well as demonstrations against Welsh language policy, apartheid, nuclear weapons, and Salman Rushdie's *Satanic Verses*, but the amount of violence on these occasions was small. Although racial tension apparently increased in, for example, Cardiff's Riverside area during these years, there was nothing to compare with the riots in the capital in 1919–20, or the troubles in Liverpool, Bristol and London in the 1980s. One result of the latter, however, was the introduction of consultative committees in the areas of mixed racial population, as recommended by Lord Scarman, and a new interest in racially motivated incidents (308 recorded in 1990). Terrorism was also only a limited threat in the south Wales police district; amongst the few cases recorded were the explosions at recruiting offices and the Welsh Office in 1981–2, and five years later, the discovery of incendiary devices planted by animal rights activists in Cardiff.

The most volatile situations facing the South Wales Constabulary in these years were undoubtedly the miners' strike and related industrial disputes of 1984–5, followed soon afterwards by the violent behaviour of the young and the unemployed. Chief Constable David East claimed that in his district, 'sensitive policing' and the reliance – except for a few days – on local officers helped to minimize the ill feeling that accompanied the miners' strike. Yet there were 479 arrests in 1984, and numerous acts of intimidation, violence and criminal damage, as attempts were made to break the strike and undermine union solidarity. The death of a taxi-driver on the Heads of the Valleys Road marked the lowest point of this confrontation.

There were, accompanying this strike, and in later years, a number of other battles with the police, involving angry workers, itinerants, and young – often unemployed – males. The years 1985–9 were notable for a series of clashes on council estates and in the city centres, when petrol bombs were thrown, cars overturned, and shops vandalized. Sometimes, the trigger for anger against the authorities was new restrictions on licensing hours, though much of the trouble was born of boredom, frustration and lack of job opportunities. The climax came in the summer of 1989, on the huge Ely estate, west Cardiff, when youths attacked the police station and caught the local and national media headlines.

Such violence, like other forms described above, was not unprecedented. In the early years of the century, assaults, disorder, and especially industrial conflicts in south Wales were also of a serious nature. Although the criminal statistics of 1969–89 indicated that crimes against the person and riotous conduct were returning to mid-Victorian levels, the reality was almost certainly different. Behaviour has generally improved over the last two hundred years, and the statistics we have been discussing partly reflect the growing intolerance of domestic and street violence since the Second World War.

Crimes against property have, by contrast, been well reported by certain classes of the population throughout the last two centuries. The resulting statistics suggest that, after a fall in the graph during the late Victorian era and low figures in the early decades of this century, the rate of property crime rose sharply after the Second World War. In recent years property has been more vulnerable than at any time since the days of Charles Dickens. During the period 1969–89 the rate of offences in the south Wales police district doubled, with the most consistent increase being in the second decade. This was the highest rate in Wales, in marked contrast to the situation regarding crimes of violence. In 1989 almost two out of three property offences in Wales were dealt with by the South Wales Constabulary. It seems unlikely that this proportion was due simply to better reporting and better policing.

The classification of property crimes has hardly changed over the last 150 years, but the returns in each category have changed significantly since the Second World War. In particular there has been a remarkable increase in the number of reported burglaries and other crimes against property committed 'with violence'. In 1938 recorded burglaries in what became the south Wales police district were 960. In 1959 the number was 3,550, and by 1969 it had risen to 13,988, with professional gangs, notorious families, and opportunist youths the main offenders. Twenty years later, after a sharp rise in the early 1980s, the number of burglaries had almost doubled, and, in the urban environment, the attacks spread ever outwards from the town centres. In 1989 break-ins amounted to almost a fifth of the value of stolen property in the district, and only 5 and 11 per cent respectively of the losses from dwelling houses and other property were recovered. For the inhabitants of Roath or Sketty, who were principal victims in our period, this was perhaps less serious than for the poorest and oldest residents of Caerau (Cardiff), Penrhys (Pontypridd), Mayhill (Swansea) and Lansbury Park (Caerphilly).

Since the 1960s, as the living and working habits of families have changed, breaking into dwellings (four out of ten break-ins) has become more common during the day as well as night-time. Compared to the situation in early modern times, the degree of violence involved has been very slight, though recently much publicity has been given to cases of pensioners being pushed aside, bound and beaten by intruders. As about one householder in twenty-five can anticipate an annual visit from a burglar, many people now live in fear of such an attack, and this has encouraged the extensive fitting of alarms and locking devices, the spread of community watch schemes, and the creation of anti-burglary squads. Perhaps this had some impact on the fall in the rate of break-ins after the mid-1980s, though another explanation was the improvement in the level of unemployment.

If the level of burglaries in south Wales since the Second World War has been unprecedented, the number of robberies has never matched that of the Dickens era. On average, fewer than 250 robberies were recorded annually during 1969–89, and the rate reached its height in the mid-1970s. They have been most common in the larger towns, especially Cardiff, and the offenders have been predominantly teenagers. Most of the offences, especially against the elderly, 'involved little more than a push and a snatch of a handbag', but there were a few exceptions. In the capital in 1987 £22,000 was taken from a post-office van, and £21,500 from two security guards delivering to a bank. The use of firearms – on 199 occasions that year, in all offences – has increased the risk of serious violence, though it is possible that the less determined robbers have recently been deterred by special street patrols and cameras in car parks and pedestrian precincts.

Much more common than robberies have been thefts, of every kind. The rate of recorded larceny and of receiving stolen goods more than doubled in our period, the fastest growth occurring during the 1980s. By 1988 the rate was twice that of the north Wales district, and only half-a-dozen police forces in England returned worse figures. There is, as has been suggested by other writers, a relationship between the incidence of such crimes, the state of the economy and unemployment, but the correlation is not a perfect one, as figures for the late 1980s indicate. Some of the thieving reminds one of the 'survival crime' of the nineteenth century. In 1989 almost half of the thefts were valued at less than £100, and included food and clothing, cash from tills and handbags, and materials from building sites. Pedal cycles, which had been favourite targets before our period, became popular again with thieves as their number and value increased. In 1989 it was estimated that losses of bicycles totalled £417,552.

Thefts by employees reported to the police in that year amounted to over a third of a million pounds in value, and we can presume that even more were ignored or dealt with outside the legal system. Workers took paper, metals, wood, fuel and much else besides. Embezzlement, fraud and forgery were sometimes one element of employee crime, but the number of reported cases of white-collar crime was never very large. Of the 2,565 frauds on the police files in 1989, many were attempts to cheat the Department of Social Security and betting companies. The fraud squad, which had less than a dozen members for half of our period, faced serious problems when dealing with the major cases involving up to £25,000,000. Extensive research was required in Companies House in Cardiff, as well as abroad, to secure an arrest in some of these cases. The fraud squad also had other tasks, tracing the source of forged banknotes and MOT certificates, and investigating corruption in local government. After years of enquiries into one case, twenty-two former councillors, officials and company directors were prosecuted in 1977 for corruption and associated offences.

Shop-lifting and car-stealing were on a different scale. The former has always been well represented on the lists of reported and prosecuted crimes, especially in the centres of Cardiff, Swansea, Pontypridd, Merthyr and Bridgend. In 1989 reported shop-lifting resulted in a loss of over a third of a million pounds, each of these offences involving goods worth, on average, £62. The rate of shop-lifting increased sharply in 1974, 1977, 1982 and 1985. The decline, from 1986 onwards, was attributed to joint management-and-police initiatives, truant patrols, and 'Stop it' campaigns. A comparison between the rate of shop-lifting, and that of stealing and taking motor vehicles without consent, is an interesting one, and gives substance to

contemporary speculation that thieves were constantly switching their attention to less defended and more expensive merchan-
dise. The rate of vehicle thefts was fairly static between 1972 and
1983, despite the increasing number of cars on the road, but then
rose dramatically. By the end of our period 'autocrime' (stealing
of and from vehicles) had become, in Cardiff and Swansea, more
than a third of recorded indictable crime. Parts of south Wales
were notorious throughout Great Britain for crimes associated
with motor vehicles, not least for the practice of 'joy-riding'. At
least forty-three motor vehicles were taken, on average, every
day in 1989 within the police district, and the cost of this,
together with thefts from cars, was set at almost £39,000,000,
or 72 per cent of the value of all stolen property.

These vehicle thefts were of a varied nature. Some were
extremely well organized, with cars and parts being moved
swiftly across country and even abroad. In the early 1970s
the stolen-vehicle police squad broke up several 'rings' of
dealers, only for them to reappear a decade later. Some of
the thefts, however, were instant decisions by one or more
youths, who passed on the vehicles for cash or used them to
ram shops and offices. In places like Tonpentre and Llanishen,
the preference was for driving the stolen cars at high speed
before dumping or burning them. 'Joy-riding' caused a number
of deaths, and brought national publicity, but these horror
stories, and the improvements in vehicle security, car park
surveillance and special police squads had, prior to 1989, only
a limited effect.

'Joy-riding' aroused such passions in south Wales partly
because it was related to other emotive forms of delinquency:
vandalism, drunken behaviour, drug abuse, and motoring
offences. Like the taking of cars, criminal damage was associated
with urban youth. About a third of those charged with the
offence were under seventeen years of age, and another third
were aged between seventeen and twenty. Changes in the law,
and the reluctance of many people to report damage of this kind,
make it impossible to describe the extent of this offence. The
impression, from literary records and police comment, is that

during the years 1969–89 the incidence of vandalism increased at a faster rate than just about any other crime, and was especially common in places such as Llanedeyrn, Fairwater, Caerau and Grangetown on the periphery of Cardiff.

A few statistics and cases convey the nature of the problem. In 1980, 5,037 incidents of criminal damage costing over £20 were recorded, and 5,867 under £20. The former amounted to an estimated £1,172,609, and nine years later the figure had risen to over £4,000,000. Common targets were building sites, boarded-up houses and shops, play areas, bus-shelters, telephone kiosks, street-lights, garages and parked cars. The frequency of national and local campaigns against vandalism, and the work of prevention panels and community policemen, highlighted the persistency of the problem. Arson, which apparently increased at the very end of our period, caused much anxiety and expense, especially when the properties were large buildings like warehouses, church and scout halls, and schools. The cost of the destruction, by two juveniles, of a large part of St Ilan's Comprehensive School, Caerphilly, in June 1989 was put at £2,000,000.

Some of these acts were committed by people under the influence of alcohol and drugs. One of the popular complaints of the time was that the level of alcoholism had increased in post-war, and comparatively affluent, society, but the criminal statistics of drunkenness – with all their limitations – have been better in the second half of this century than they were a hundred years ago. During 1969–89 the figures for court cases of simple drunkenness and drunken and disorderly behaviour rose from 1,371 to 2,813, peaking in the early 1980s. Since then, considerable efforts have been made, by the police and others, to reduce under-age drinking, to limit the opening hours of night-clubs, wine-bars and dance-halls, and to control the menace of drunken hooligans in the streets.

The danger of drug abuse evoked an even more varied response. It was a growing problem, and one largely particular to the period. In 1970 only 274 persons were charged with offences involving drugs in the police district. Cannabis was then the most favoured drug, though concern was growing about LSD and heroin. Twenty years later, cannabis was still popular, amphetamines had become so, but 'crack' was not yet a problem. In 1989, 1,084 persons were arrested for drug-related offences, 821 persons were stopped and searched on suspicion of possessing illegal drugs, and 328 warrants were issued under the Misuse of Drugs Act (1971).

The illicit trade in drugs required considerable planning and organization. In some instances this amounted to forging prescriptions, and stealing from local doctors' cars and pharmacies; in others, dealers had to obtain their goods from elsewhere in Britain and abroad. Drugs arrived via London, Southampton and the docks and airports of south Wales. In 1981, operating with the Metropolitan police, the South Wales Constabulary successfully broke up three major drugs organizations. At the same time, the police and the wider community put greater efforts into prevention, for these years were marked not just by experiments with new and more dangerous drugs, but also by the phenomenon of solvent abuse. In the early 1980s there were deaths in Pontypridd and Swansea induced by sniffing noxious substances, and action committees and educational projects were launched in quick succession.

It was widely recognized that the statistics of drug-related offences bore no relationship to the size of the problem. 'If more police resources were available', said a Pontypridd police officer in 1987, 'many more offences would be detected.' The same point was made concerning motoring offences, which have become the largest group of crimes dealt with by the courts and the police. In 1970 there were 9,146 proceedings over exceeding the speed limit, 4,799 for dangerous and careless driving, and 28,774 for obstruction and parking offences. Only a very small proportion of these cases were treated like the others in this chapter, as serious or indictable crimes. By 1989 the number of recorded offences relating to motor vehicles, including those punished by fixed penalties, had trebled, and there was an even bigger increase in the number of drink-driving cases. In short, the last quarter of this century has seen, because of motoring offences, the criminalization of the population at an exceptional rate.

Despite this, the term 'criminal' in 1989 was still used in a narrower sense, to describe those people who have committed several offences against people and property. Those appearing regularly in the courts for such crimes in the years 1969–89 were mainly of the working class, and disproportionately from the ranks of the unemployed and the poorly paid. The ages of those found guilty of indictable offences varied somewhat over this period, and across communities, but typically half were under twenty-one years of age, and a quarter under seventeen years. This participation of children and youths in crime has been a feature of the post-war years, and the complaints at Cardiff conferences in 1941 and 1950 about juvenile recidivism, poor parenting and truancy levels became even louder during the 1980s and early 1990s.

On reflection, therefore, it seems that by 1989 many of the hopes raised when the south Wales police district was created had not been fulfilled. The rate of increase in indictable crime, a feature of the post-war years, hardly slackened. According to the police figures of 1989, the district was still a comparatively safe place in which to live, though reports of serious violence, attacks on the police and the drug problem did increase significantly. In a longer historical context, the level of such disorder was not exceptional, nor were the rates of some property crimes like robbery, petty theft, stealing at work and shop-lifting. However, the continued – if slower – increase in break-ins in the years 1969–89, and the unprecedented rise in thefts of vehicles, undoubtedly heightened the anxiety felt by many groups in society, and reduced the general tolerance and understanding of criminal behaviour. Fear was now matched by experience; each year, at the end of the period, at least one family in three in south Wales became the victim of some kind of indictable crime.

Much of the blame for the worsening crime rate since amalgamation has been placed, often unfairly, on the police. The level of policing increased during the 1970s, but the ratio of officers to population was static in the 1980s, when the detection rate, once the pride of the force, gradually fell. All the many changes in Home Office policy, local police management and crime prevention during the period had, it now appears, no obvious influence on the overall rate of offences, though there were some successes in containing individual crimes. Much is expected, long term, of the community policing begun in the early 1980s, but the hopes of an older experiment, unit beat policing, are still ruefully remembered. In the 1980s, confronted by renewed media attention, increased public anxiety and reporting, and a government obsessed with administrative reforms, economy and performance, it would be surprising if the 'men in blue' were not somewhat defensive and ready to highlight the need for other than simple policing solutions to complex social problems. Altogether, it will be interesting to see how Home Secretaries and Chief Constables respond to the challenges of the next twenty years.

Bibliographical note

I am grateful, for assistance in preparing this chapter, to Margaret Ayres of the Home Office Research and Statistics Department at Croydon, Natalie Aye Maung of the Home Office Research and Planning Department in London, Chief Constable Robert Lawrence, Chief Superintendent Brian Meredith, and especially Jeremy Glenn, Curator of the South Wales Police Museum, and Sharon Davies. Mr Glenn gave me invaluable advice on sources, and read the first draft of the chapter. The major sources are the annual Command Papers of Criminal Statistics, England and Wales, followed, after 1980, by the more detailed annual Supplementary Tables, published by the Government Statistical Service. To these must be added the Annual Reports of the Chief Constable of the South Wales Constabulary (from which the quotations were taken), Establishment Reviews, 1972–86 (seen by permission at Police Headquarters, Bridgend), and reports of crime in the *Western Mail* and local newspapers. Because of the limitation of space, the story of non-indictable crime has been largely excluded from this chapter. For a comparative Welsh study on crime prior to 1969, see D. J. V. Jones, '"Where did it all go wrong?": Crime in Swansea, 1938–68', *The Welsh History Review*, XV, 2, 1990. On the social geography and sociology of this crime, ignored for want of space, see the many publications of

Professors David Herbert and David Smith, such as D. T. Herbert, *The Geography of Urban Crime* (London, 1982), and D. T. Herbert and D. M. Smith (eds.), *Social Problems and the City* (London, 1989). To put the police statistics in perspective, see the work of M. Hough, P. Mayhew, and others since their *The British Crime Survey* (London, 1983).

2

Voices of the Unheard: Contemporary British Urban Riots in Historical Perspective

NEIL EVANS

Serious urban riots have flashed across our television screens and elbowed their way into political discussion for most of the period since 1979. However, fully convincing analysis remains elusive. It might seem impertinent for a historian to intrude into contemporary concerns, but from the beginning of the current round of riots the search for explanation has involved an appeal to the past. The first was the anguished cry of outraged Thatcherism. What were the poor coming to? Such violence had never happened before in Britain, a society which had been characterized by civil peace. In the 1930s the unemployed had not rioted but got on their bikes and gone in search of work. This view was quickly refuted by historians. There was a long line of riots in the British past. Indeed, historians were much in demand as commentators on the 1980–81 riots simply because they had some (admittedly indirect) experience of the phenomenon. For almost thirty years before the Bristol outbreak of 1980, historians had been finding a significant role for 'the crowd in history'. There had even been a proposal for a separate sub-discipline of crowd history.

The common responses to the riots of 1981 were remarkably like those of the eighteenth century. The authorities denounced both as the work of criminals, agitators, and of people generally sunk into the depths of immorality. More reasoned and informed analysis found that they were like the riots of the past in that they had clear causes – the racist policing of British inner cities and the first Thatcher recession were the most widely canvassed. Closer study found them to be as discriminating in their targets as those of the past. In Bristol the rioters confined themselves to controlling their own territory and expelling the police from it; they observed a strictly demarcated boundary, and shopping and most aspects of everyday life continued, riot or not. Police vehicles and a bank were prime targets. In Brixton a pub which allegedly refused to serve blacks was burned out, while an anarchist bookshop was spared. In Toxteth the well-heeled Racquets Club, where judges who condemned local people to prison sentences recuperated from the task, was a prime target. The Rialto's days as a dance-hall, when it had barred blacks, were recalled while it was torched, while a furniture warehouse belonging to an unpopular Tory politician was another target. Bystanders felt no sense of danger. One woman remarked: 'We weren't frightened because we knew just what people were going for.'[1]

This was no more uncontrolled than when the Gordon Rioters in 1780 had spared the dwellings of poor Catholics, the better to concentrate their anger on rich ones. Thus, in the 1980s, riots came to be seen as a resurgence of an older phenomenon. It was around this time, too, that the race riots in British cities in 1919 were rediscovered, and they provided another context in which the events of the early eighties could be placed. Simon Winchester presented a *Chronicle* programme in 1982 which suggested that the tradition went back to the pre-industrial food riot, and was unbroken through to 1980–81. By 1991 a journalist could observe almost casually: 'Riots and insurrections have been part of the British political scene for most of the past 900 years. There have been at least 100 violent rebellions over those nine centuries.'[2]

As a shorthand account of the past, this was clearly more realistic than Thatcherite incantations of evil. Yet it also foreclosed the past and reduced the illumination which it is possible to gain from historical studies. Contemporary riots are not unprecedented, but neither are they exactly the same as those of the past. Patterns can be detected in the past and these show what is distinctive about the current scene.

The pioneer historian of the crowd was George Rudé. In a variety of works published in the 1950s and early 1960s he laid the basis for a novel approach which many others would follow.[3] His conclusions were clear. Crowds were almost always composed of middle-aged, non-criminal, established people; they had distinct targets and values. They were not less rational than individuals within them were. Leaders tended to emerge from the crowd; there were no conspiracies lying behind them. They were decisive in their shaping influence on history in the period *c.* 1730–1848 and essentially they were a stage in the evolution of the labour movement. The crowd and the corn riot were dominant in the eighteenth century, but they gave way inexorably to the trade union and the strike as the nineteenth century progressed. Another way of expressing this was the idea of 'collective bargaining by riot', first elaborated by Eric Hobsbawm. Episodes like machine-breaking were not so much resistance to machines, but ways in which workers could exert pressure upon their employers.

Eventually flaws were detected in this analysis. Rudé ended his interest in the phenomenon with the European Revolutions of 1848. Others found the riot was a very persistent form of social action. It simply changed its form. Food riots, the dominant form of social protest in the eighteenth century, were supposed to give way to modern forms of action like trade unions and political parties in the early nineteenth century. In fact, the riot proved to be a protean form of social action. The demise of the food riot was found to be greatly exaggerated. Scotland had a significant outbreak in 1848, Liverpool had riots in 1855, and the most intrepid chronicler found disturbances over potatoes during the rationing of the First World War. Election riots were also stubborn, and not really eradicated until the 1880s. A study of Croydon found violent crowd actions persisting until the 1890s. This meant that 'primitive rebels' overlapped with the violent actions associated with the rise of 'modern' social movements like political parties and trade unions. Violent activity was used by *unionized* workers in the Sheffield cutlery trades and the Manchester brick-making trades into the 1850s and 1860s. The first agitations of the unemployed in the 1880s, orchestrated by the Social Democratic Federation, frequently led to riots, as in Trafalgar Square and Pall Mall in 1886 and 1887.

Fear of this urban mass, it seems, led to some relief in the City that nothing worse came out of the dockers' agitation of 1889 than a trade union and a 6d. increase in wages. But not all the experience of the new unionism of 1889–92 was to be so peaceful. The connection between trade unionism and violence was even closer in the next 'explosion' of organization amongst the unskilled in 1910–14. Where the London dock strike of 1889 had been noted for its peaceful marches, the tone of 1912 was very different. At a meeting on Tower Hill in the 1912 dock strike, Ben Tillett invoked the aid of the deity: 'God strike Lord Devonport dead!', he exclaimed, seeking vengeance on the head of the Port of London Authority. The emergence of the labour movement in the early twentieth century was frequently marked by violence, and Jane Morgan demonstrated brilliantly the way in which this had ramifications into the whole system of policing. Troops were frequently drafted into policing roles, central control over police forces increased, and Chief Constables had their authority enhanced at the cost of reduced democratic control.

Much of this riot paralleled earlier outbreaks. Crowds attacked the shops in Tonypandy High Street just as the privations of the Cambrian Combine strike were beginning to bite, in search of the luxuries of life which they were now being denied. People paraded the streets in cheap finery looted from the smashed windows. Shopkeepers seemed to be the class enemy: they increasingly lined up with the coalowners. As with food riots there was selectivity; the premises of a rugby hero were left unscathed: no one who had played for Wales in the epic victory over the All Blacks in 1905 could be the class enemy! All through the strike there were attempts at collective bargaining by violence – stopping the pumps to bring the coalowners to the bargaining table. There were parallel outbreaks at Llanelli in the following year during the national railway strike; similar looting, similar selectivity. A little earlier in the year the seamen's strike had been marked in Cardiff by three distinct outbreaks of riot; one by dockers who objected to the unloading by scab labour of a cargo which they had 'blacked' in solidarity with the seamen; another against the property of Chinese who were regarded as being blacklegs in the dispute; and finally, there were attacks on the accommodation of the hated Metropolitan Police – sent into Cardiff to keep 'order', they had become a menace to it with their unprovoked attacks on citizens.

In many ways this was not collective bargaining by riot, so much as riots in pursuit of collective bargaining. It was a huge shove aimed at creating institutions of economic democracy. Some of this persisted into the inter-war period, though the tendency was for the strikers to become less violent, and for the police to be the instigators of incidents. This was true of most of the violence associated with strikes and unemployed demonstrations in the inter-war period. Yet contrary to the Thatcher/Tebbitt myth there were also unemployed riots in the thirties – at Belfast in 1932, where shots were fired by the police and the issue was strong enough to breach sectarian boundaries, uniting workers against the means test. There were also two days of violence at Birkenhead in 1932, and similar conflicts in North Shields. In south Wales in 1935 there was the largest demonstration ever seen in the valleys, which culminated in the sacking of the Unemployment Assistance Board offices in Merthyr. There were also many minor outbreaks on the streets of the valleys as people resisted bailiffs, fascists, and company unionists. In the index of the *Western Mail* the heading 'Riot' makes an appearance in the 1930s, so frequent were these outbreaks in south Wales.

Britain therefore has a plentiful history of riot before the Second World War, and there is no obvious point at which one can safely say that working-class violence had been 'tamed'. Of course, its record is rather less violent than that of the United States and France, as Jane Morgan was at pains to emphasize. Some places within Britain had strong local traditions: Belfast is notorious and too extreme a case for it to bear any general weight. So is Liverpool; in the nineteenth century it had enough anti-Irish riots to fill a good-sized modern scholarly account. Between 1909 and 1919 it experienced no fewer than five major riots. There was Protestant/Catholic communal violence in 1909 and again in the transport strike of 1911. In 1915 German shops were attacked after the sinking of the *Lusitania*; in June 1919 there were attacks on the homes and property of black sailors. One black man died after he was pushed into the dock. Within weeks, during the police strike, the residents of Scotland Road took the opportunity for free pickings from the unprotected shops. Four of the riots (the race riots seem to be the exception) were the work of the slum dwellers of the north end of the city.[4] Cardiff can also muster a substantial history of riot. There was a serious anti-Irish riot in 1848, innumerable street disturbances between rival ethnic groups of sailors, almost as many against the new police force before they could establish their authority, as well as a severe election riot in 1886, the disturbances during the 1911 strike referred to above, and the worst race riot of the whole British outbreak of 1919, in which three men died. To finish the story there were disturbances between unemployed demonstrators and the police in both 1921 and 1931.

How different is the picture in post-war Britain? Political demonstrations from the 1960s onwards, and the escalating industrial disputes of the 1970s – those of 1970–74 surpassed those of 1910–14 on the statistical indices – became associated with outbreaks of public disorder. Many riots were related to race in some way or other. If anyone remembers a riot before those of the last decade or so it is likely to be the disturbances in Notting Hill and Nottingham in 1958 that are recalled. Similar disturbances in Middlesbrough three years later are now being uncovered. In style they were similar to the outbreaks of 1919 – white attacks on black newcomers. They paralleled a style of riot found in America from before the First World War until the great Detroit and Harlem riots of 1943. American riots began to change then and did so decisively in the sixties with the coming of the massive ghetto rebellions in Newark, Watts (Los Angeles), and many other cities. It was these that Martin

Luther King called the 'voice of the unheard', characterized by explosions of black anger over ghetto conditions and policing. The British riots of the early 1980s were largely scaled down versions of this new American style, though there were also important differences between them.[5]

The Bristol riot of 1980 was followed by more widespread disturbances in 1981 and 1985. Virtually all these riots had a racial element within them. That is not to say that all the crowds were composed of black people, but virtually everywhere the long-standing conflict between local communities and the police was at the heart of the matter. Those who have played down this aspect have tended to point to deprivation as an alternative explanation. It does not hold enough water to be convincing. Areas like the north-east of England were more deprived on the statistical indices than rioting inner cities, but were nevertheless peaceful. Glasgow should have rioted if deprivation was a fully independent variable. The relative absence of a West Indian population ensured that it did not. Women have rarely been rioters, though their deprivation is often greater than that of men. Riot-prone areas were both deprived *and* the focus of clashes between local youths and the police.[6] The Special Patrol Group had been deployed in Brixton four times before the outbreak there; the situation *before* the riot has been described as 'war'. On top of this, the community was involved in a campaign to direct the attention of the police to a fire in Deptford in which a number of black people had died. Brixton thought they were the victims of a racist attack; the police did not. Toxteth had a similarly difficult history and even a Conservative member of the Merseyside police committee thought that the Chief Constable was arrogant.

The riots fitted into a pattern of emerging politicization in black communities. In Bristol, older Rastafarians emerged as leaders during the riots. Brixton was the home of the journal *Race Today* and generally the ideas of black pride were taking root amongst the British-born youth. Southall had been mobilized in 1979 to resist provocative marches by the National Front and it was to be a skinhead invasion (rather than a police action) which precipitated its violence in 1981. The resistance was rooted in a decade-and-a-half's industrial action in the community as well as its experiences in the Anti-Nazi League in the 1970s. Generally it drew on the forms which the politically conscious would have been familiar with – the American ghetto rebellions of the sixties and the street actions in Ulster which were regularly beamed into sitting rooms throughout Britain.[7]

Urban riots returned to Britain in 1985 with a new and deadlier force. In Handsworth, relatively untouched in 1981, two Asian shopkeepers died when their shop was burned. In Tottenham's Broadwater Farm Estate, PC Keith Blakelock was hacked to death by a crowd, and shots were fired. Police armed with baton rounds were deployed for the first time in mainland Britain though they did not use their weapons. Again the issues revolved around the policing of black communities and the continuing effects of the recession upon them. Handsworth had been held up as the example of community policing to be emulated in the 1981 outbreaks. Its disturbances had been relatively small and readily contained. By 1985 that policy had been reversed, and police and shopkeepers reaped the whirlwind. In Tottenham it was another insensitive action by the police – the death of Cynthia Jarret during a search of her home – which sowed the seeds of violence. Things were taking a particularly worrying turn: if there was escalation in future outbreaks, killing fields of American proportions seemed to be on the agenda.

In the event, black communities seemed to have found means of expressing their grievances in the more orthodox political arena. Bernie Grant became famous for fifteen minutes for saying that the police had got a 'good hiding' at Broadwater Farm, but it is more significant that two years later he became MP for the area and a symbol of the achievements of black politics. In all, four black MPs were returned in 1987, the first black people into the House of Commons since the 1920s. This paralleled the campaign for black sections in the Labour Party and arose from the wider political mobilization of black communities, referred to above. They had a historical and international framework into which they could fit their experiences: in 1979 a Punjabi newspaper had compared the resistance of the community to the National Front with the Amritsar Massacre. The parallel is perhaps a little forced, but it vividly illustrates the intellectual world into which the resistance of black communities could be fitted. The riots have been a challenge to the more complacent and established black leadership. The new organization comes from blacks who have grown up in Britain, who have no colonial myths of Britain's tolerance to burden themselves with, and who have experienced racism from birth.

When riots returned to the cities in 1991–2 they had dramatically changed their location.[8] They were again related to recession though not exclusively explained by it. The sweeping changes introduced in social security in 1988 are a crucial context. Youths of sixteen to eighteen years of age were deprived of benefit, and emergency payments were replaced by the loans of the so-called Social Fund. Overall, there has been a massive shift in the distribution of wealth away from the poor; in real terms they were 14 per cent worse off in 1990–91 than when Mrs Thatcher came to power.[9] The outbreaks affected predominantly white communities – in Cardiff they were in white Ely rather than black Butetown. The locale was now the peripheral urban estates rather than the inner city; the rioters were chiefly white rather than black, and it was much harder to connect the outbreaks with any kind of political struggle. The targets were less clear. In some the tinge of racism was to be seen. In Cardiff the outbreak was precipitated by the attempt of an Asian shopkeeper to enforce a restrictive covenant which prevented the adjoining (white-owned) shop from encroaching on its trade. The violence which followed seemed to be rooted in resentment at what the Asian shopkeeper had achieved. Ely has a black minority population but had also been the location of some British National Party activity. The racist band White Storm (who were killed in a car crash on the way to playing at a far-right gathering) came from Ely. On Tyneside there were similar strands. Asian shops on the Meadowell estate were

burned despite the fact that their owners lived above them, and
there were similar threats to black property in the riots which
followed in the West End of Newcastle. In this respect some of
the disturbances were scaled-down versions of the anti-black
riots of 1919–61.

Yet they were less coherent overall, though hostility to the
police was a fairly constant factor. In Ely the police quickly
displaced the shopkeeper as the focus of violence. At Meadowell
events centred on the attempt to wreak vengeance on the police
for their alleged (and almost certainly non-existent) role in
chasing car thieves who spun out of control and died in the
ensuing blaze. These were areas which the police had given up
on, rather than those which were the subject of massive and
unwelcome attentions that black communities had received in
the 1970s and 80s. Many residents would have welcomed a
stronger police presence to ease the pressures exerted by local
criminals on their lives. The burning of public buildings on the
Meadowell estate was clearly an attempt by the white youth
groups to lure the police into an ambush, and the tactic was
repeated elsewhere over the next few weeks. Yet this was
anger and resentment that was much less clearly directed than
that of the black communities had been in the early 1980s.
Often, local shops and community facilities were torched and
in many ways what happened was simply an amplification of
the normally riotous and criminal behaviour of young men in
these areas. It was a civil war in which local residents did
sometimes feel worried for their safety, though apparently at
Ely the disturbances became a spectator sport: 'Coming up
the riot?' was the invitation that was offered. It is hard to
connect any of this with a political standpoint: one observer
of Meadowell thought that the politics that would make any
sense to the rioters is the rather incoherent anger of class war.
This violence was not entirely undirected: the first building to
be burned was a community centre closed in local authority
cuts. It was probably singled out by the council because of the
role which parts of the estate (the women active in community
politics rather then the young men who rioted) played in the

anti-poll-tax campaign. This meant they became a target of the ruling Labour group as (by association) supporters of the Militant Tendency.

The break with the riots of the early eighties was not absolute. The form of the disturbances owed much to the example of the earlier outbreaks, and deprivation and policing were common themes. Historians have argued that crowds develop repertoires of actions in specific historical periods. The inner-city riots made transferable forms available for the outer estate eruptions. There had also been some outbreaks on peripheral estates in the early 1980s and white youths had been involved then, though largely as looters rather than at the leading edge of the conflict.[10] Yet contrasts abound: the latest outbreaks require a different vocabulary. Terry Davis has provided an excellent typology of racial violence and in his terms the disturbances of 1980–85 seem to be examples of 'political conflict'; actions of groups contending for power and influence. Those of 1991–2 seem to be more inchoate examples of 'civil disorder' – marginal people with no connection with corporate structures of power, capable of a hostile outburst but of no coherent political strategy. The unheard voices of 1980–85 were speaking more coherently than those of 1991–2.[11]

In contrast to a long history of disorder in Britain these latest riots come closest to matching the establishment image of violence being the product of young, criminal and rootless people. Something significant is happening to Britain in that we cannot fit the riots of our time into a seamless British history of crowd action. Much of the current discussion of British urban riots is questionable in the light of the historical evidence. It has been common to link the recent disturbances in white communities with a decline in working-class culture. The weakening hold of institutions – churches, trade unions, social clubs, etc., is seen as a backdrop to the disturbances. Once there was a working-class culture which gave people hope – and an alternative to riot.[12] The main problem with the argument is that it is wrong. Riots in the past were more likely to come out of organized communities than out of disorganized ones. Artisans with fraternities, trade unions and a strong sense of craft identity were more likely rioters than the displaced, wandering poor. This seems to be true at least up to the First World War and probably to the General Strike of 1926. After that working-class culture may have become more defensive, but in the early nineteenth century – and from 1880 to 1920 – there is a clear sense of forward movement, and violence and riot had a role within this. Working-class communities aided this process rather than retarded it, though they could also express their solidarity as a hostility to outsiders. 'We are all at one in Newport', exclaimed a rioter in 1919, 'and intend to clear these niggers out.' It would be more accurate to say that working-class community provided a more focused and directed social violence than many contemporary outbreaks.

Other contemporary analysis rests on shaky historical foundations. Jock Young asserts that the insurgents of 1991-2 are the first of the non-starving to riot. They are after the consumer durables which life on the dole is denying them.[13] This would be better turned on its head. Historically, these are the *first* of the very poor to riot if we understand poverty to be relative to conditions in contemporary society. Rioters in the past were not the worst off in general terms but the better-off working class. The food rioter was not so much hungry as in fear of hunger. In the 1790s in south Wales the food rioters were the skilled copper workers of Swansea and the iron workers of Merthyr, groups in the vanguard of the industrial revolution rather than victims of technological change. There was much discussion in the early and mid nineteenth century of the evils threatened by the 'dangerous classes': much of it is similar to present discussions of the 'underclass'. Yet, generally, it was not the 'dangerous' class that rioted in the nineteenth-century but those above them in the scale. If what we know about nineteenth-century America is any guide, one of the reasons for this was that economic failure in the nineteenth century implied constant movement in search of work. The situation was the reverse of the present when the rich are mobile and it is the losers who remain locked within their communities.

What is happening in the inner cities is not a replay of the nineteenth century. It represents a new historical phase, and the past has not been used adequately to analyse it. Approaching this issue leads us into the identification of the 'underclass'. In its original usage this term designated structural poverty within western industrial societies; those who had no chance of advancement because of economic and social structures. It has more recently shifted to become an explanation of poverty: the poor are those with moral defects which make them unable to survive in modern society. It is probably impossible to remove the taint which now attaches to the term because of recent discussion, but we need to retain the idea of a group of people who have been driven into a peculiarly disadvantaged position.

There is some contemporary discussion of the idea of a two-thirds/one-third society; that is, one in which the relatively affluent are enough of a majority to exclude the concerns of the remainder from the political agenda. Clearly, industrial areas of Britain are victims of the globalization of production and have lost jobs to the Newly Industrialized Countries. The welfare systems, which have put a safety net under the working class in most Western countries since the turn of the century, are being challenged in Britain. A strong factor in shaping these was 'social imperialism' – the competition between a group of industrial countries which challenged each other for control and dominance of the world market. None felt it could compete effectively unless it mobilized its human capital. This situation no longer obtains. Capital goes in search of the cheapest labour it can find, and frequently outside of national boundaries. Some European social policy flies in the face of this by trying to provide welfare rights for the whole population. The British government is seeking to escape from these and to make up for inadequacies of investment and government economic policies by making Britain compete with lower wages and limited welfare benefits. 'Social dumping' is one of the few long-range strategies that it has. Thatcherite housing policies have emphasized the distinctiveness of the British 'underclass'. The drive to reduce the level of state provision of housing has stigmatized those who remain in such housing in a way unthinkable in the past. As a way of introducing themselves at the start of the 1988 TV series 'The Divided Kingdom', three of the five presenters chose to go back to the council houses in which they had been brought up. For them the house represented the first rung up the ladder that had led them on to grammar school, university and television stardom. No one will want to – or be able to – do that about Moss Side or Broadwater Farm in the future. Such areas have reputations like nineteenth-century rookeries and it would be against all the odds if they liberated anyone.

In the absence of a coherent social and economic policy which would redress the grievances under which rioters suffer, there has been a predictable resort to tougher policing. The traditions of the British police – at least on the mainland and outside the Empire – have required at least lip service to be paid to the idea of consent. The Scarman Report on the Brixton disturbances of 1981 reasserted this with its criticisms of police behaviour and its advocacy of community policing. Amongst the long-term causes of the riotous cities of our time are the changes in policing introduced from the 1960s as a consequence of the advent of the two-way radio and the panda car. The style of 'fire brigade' policing which developed did not allow for much rapport between the police and the policed. The impact of the riots has amplified this trend. Almost immediately after the 1981 outbreaks, tactics were imported from the imperial tradition of the promiscuous deployment of force against a subject population rather than the control by consent of fellow citizens. Baton rounds, snatch squads and riot gear were imported from Hong Kong, though some of the methods had been honed in Northern Ireland along the way. By 1992 the police were equipped like Robocop and could switch in an instant from their day-by-day role to a paramilitary force. The new methods were deployed in the Miners' Strike and at Wapping, though it was the eruption of the inner city which had occasioned the switch. It was accompanied by another twist in the central theme of police history – growing central control combined with removal from any effective local and democratic supervision. By the end of the 1980s it was a matter of concern to civil libertarians:

> ... every plastic bullet or CS gas cannister fired in a British city will be a shot in the dark. It could prove fatal not only for those at the scene, but ultimately for the police tradition which Britain has pioneered.[14]

This is not a conclusion with which Jane would have been comfortable. She would have recognized it as an extension of the process she charted so lucidly and powerfully in *Conflict and Order*. At present we have the police turning themselves into a paramilitary force rather than the employing of the army in the same role as was the case earlier in the century. The modern lack of responsibility of Chief Constables to elected civil authority is now buttressed by the discipline imposed on individual Chief Constables by the Home Office and the Association of Chief Police Officers. *Conflict and Order* is a humane book, driven by a concern for civil liberties and democracy. We are all the poorer that its author is no longer with us to apply her sensitivity and intellect to the problems that the current situation creates.

Notes

This is an essay, not a work of research, and I have not over-burdened it with references: in particular I have given few references to historical works. David Byrne of the University of Durham kindly spent a morning explaining Meadowell and West Newcastle to me, and I read the cuttings in Newcastle's excellent Central Library on these incidents. I also used cuttings I have accumulated on the riots more generally, and discussed growing up in Ely with my student, Monique Ennis, who had perceptive things to say about the experience. Otherwise, my sources are secondary and I have indicated my indebtedness only to the most central of them. My colleagues, Sue Chamberlain and Dai Michael, have given me a host of relevant references and greatly helped me by their readiness to discuss these matters.

1 Martin Kettle and Lucy Hodges, *Uprising: the Police, the People and the Riots in Britain's Cities* (London, 1982); S. D. Reicher, 'The St Paul's Riot: An Explanation of the Limits of Crowd Action

in Terms of a Social Identity Model', *European Journal of Social Psychology*, Vol. 14 (1984); P. J. Waller, 'The Riots in Toxteth, Liverpool: A Survey', *New Community*, Vol. IX No. 3 (Winter 1981/Spring 1982).

2 *Independent*, 10 March 1990.

3 George Rudé, *The Crowd in History* (London and New York, 1964) is the most convenient source of his views.

4 R. Merfyn Jones, 'The Dangerous City: Liverpool's History of Social Disorder' (unpublished paper, 1987).

5 Simon Field and Peter Southgate, *Public Disorder: A Review of Research and a Study in One Inner City Area* (Home Office Research Study No. 72, HMSO, 1982). Martin Luther King's saying is sometimes quoted as 'the language of the unheard'.

6 Ceri Peach, 'A Geographical Perspective on the 1981 Urban Riots in England', *Ethnic and Racial Studies*, Vol. 9 (No. 3, July 1986).

7 John Rex, 'The 1981 Urban Riots in Britain', *International Journal of Urban and Regional Research*, Vol. 6 (Part 1, 1982); Campaign Against Racism and Facism/Southall Rights, *Southall: The Birth of a Black Community* (London, 1981).

8 Beatrix Campbell, *Goliath: Britain's Dangerous Places* (London, 1993).

9 *Guardian*, 3 April 1992; 1 July 1993.

10 Paul Cooper, 'Competing Explanations of the Merseyside Riots of 1981', *British Journal of Criminology*, Vol. 25 (No. 1, January 1985).

11 Terry Davis, 'The Forms of Collective Racial Violence', *Political Studies*, Vol. XXXIV (No. 1, March 1986).

12 Richard Hoggart in *Independent on Sunday*, 29 September 1991.

13 Jock Young, in *Independent on Sunday*, 19 July 1992.

14 Gerry Northam, *Shooting in the Dark: Riot Police in Britain* (London, 1988) p.157; for Robocop see, *Independent on Sunday*, 15 September 1991.

3

Lloyd George and Churchill: What Difference Did They Make?

PETER CLARKE

Lloyd George and Churchill ostensibly led Britain to victory in two world wars. Both exemplify the 'heroic' style of political leadership. Arguably the most charismatic British prime ministers of the present century, neither was impregnable. The greater the pretensions of a leader, the more stunning the fate which hubris holds in store for him – or her. For a moment after the First World War, Lloyd George looked like the master of Europe – until a meeting of Conservative back-benchers in 1922 pulled the rug from under his coalition government. Churchill's wartime grand strategy paid off in 1945, only for its architect to be summarily dismissed by the British electorate. This essay makes use of some recent publications on twentieth-century British history which offer revisionist perspectives on their careers. By examining their careers I hope to illustrate the role of leadership in seizing – or missing – opportunities to influence the course of politics.

Leadership needs to be understood in a broad sense. There are two obvious criteria. The first is setting the agenda of politics by determining which issues dominate political argument and shape the role of government. The big issues in modern British politics have changed in each generation in this way. The other task of leadership is that of mobilizing political support, a problem which has been tackled at various levels in modern Britain. At an executive level, it has turned on controlling the structure of government, whether through the constitutional channel of the cabinet or through mastery of the civil service machine in Whitehall. At a legislative level it has reflected the British premium on gladiatorial combat in the parliamentary forum at Westminster, reinforced by control of party organization. At an electoral level, it has implied an appeal to public opinion, which in turn implies making use of the communications media.

We need to ask how far these leaders had a vision of politics which they hoped to impose as the agenda of government. We need to examine how far their efforts in mobilizing support – whether through power struggles at the top or through appeals to public opinion – were driven by opportunism and personal ambition. And we need to ask, in the end, what difference did they make?

Some historians, of course, dismiss the role of personality as trivial in affecting the course of politics. In criticizing my own work, Eric Hobsbawm has made this point with characteristic trenchancy:

> Contrary to what is held by believers in the cult of personality, who range from newspaper editors to political historians, it may make very little difference . . . [Clarke] is a sufficiently sophisticated historian to appreciate the force of structural explanations which 'emphasise what was likely to happen – on the whole, in the long run, in one guise or another', irrespective of the intentions of the actors or their ability to carry them out . . . On the other hand, Clarke retreats from broad explanations by opting for 'contingent' ones – for the kind of history 'which needs to recapture the complex play of causation in specific instances', so that we can understand, not what was likely or unlikely to happen, but 'what actually happened in particular'. This is not necessarily of great historical significance . . .[1]

Hobsbawm rightly mentions that I make a distinction between 'structural' and 'contingent' explanations but I am unable to accept that opting for one or the other, as appropriate, in making sense of different historical factors, is simply a 'retreat'; and I am likewise unable to accept Hobsbawm's kind commiserations for having wasted my time on an unworthy subject.

Let us agree that the virtue of structural explanations is that they are susceptible of generalization. Yet contingent explanations are also necessary to account for what happens in particular. The methodological point can be made by reference to a celebrated illustration given by E. H. Carr:

> Jones, returning from a party at which he has consumed more than his usual ration of alcohol, in a car whose brakes turn out to have been defective, at a blind corner where visibility is notoriously poor, knocks down and kills Robinson, who was crossing the road to buy cigarettes at the shop on the corner.[2]

Clearly there are many ways in which the cause of the accident can be described – including the fact that Robinson would not have been crossing the road had he not desired to buy some cigarettes. Carr suggests that there is no difficulty, however, in recognizing which are the 'rational' explanations. They are those from which we can learn lessons, like curbing the consumption of alcohol by drivers, or testing the condition of brakes, or improving the siting of roads; all these might serve to reduce road accidents, whereas reducing the general level of smoking would not have such an effect. Hence Carr's distinction between rational and accidental causes. 'Accidental causes cannot be generalized; and, since they are in the fullest sense of the word unique, they teach no lessons and lead to no conclusions.'[3] This may be a useful maxim in constructing theoretical sciences on the basis of abstraction in order to yield general hypotheses. Yet suppose it is the death of *Robinson* which is the question? In that case, we may need to invoke the general in order to understand the particular, for it is the particular which historians often need to understand.

Take a real historical example. On 10 August 1945, following the bombing of Hiroshima four days earlier, the second atomic bomb was dropped by the United States Air Force on the Mitsubishi steelworks in Nagasaki. Why? To bring about the end of the Second World War, or to hasten an already inevitable Japanese surrender, or to pre-empt Soviet participation in this theatre, or to seize the opportunity of using a new weapon in which competitive reputations as well as massive resources had been invested – many pertinent arguments can be generated along such lines, leading to far-reaching hypotheses about strategic imperatives and the politics of military technology. Yet there is another line of causation, interlocking with the first, which would invoke completely different facts: that Nagasaki was only added to the list of four Japanese targets in place of Kyoto, which War Secretary Stimson, with his pre-war nostalgia for the old capital, vetoed; that Kokkura, the target selected after the Hiroshima raid, was under cloud cover when the bomber flew over; that in Nagasaki itself the Mitsubishi shipyard was also obscured by clouds; but that the steelworks briefly appeared in the bomb-sights, just when the aircraft's fuel supply was near its limit for a safe return to base . . .[4] This line of historical explanation can hardly be called trivial in its effects upon the people of Nagasaki.

These are not competitive but complementary types of explanation in addressing the complexity of real life. What is contingent at one historical moment becomes locked into the historical process, to that extent determining its whole course, so as to become part of the structural conditions which constrain future options. The conclusion that small causes may generate very considerable consequences is a truism because it carries a time-worn truth. Indeed, as Geoffrey Hawthorn has demonstrated with exemplary rigour, it may be possible to isolate the crucial moment at which equally realistic and undetermined alternatives were historically accessible; even though the path to these plausible worlds was then foreclosed by the subsequent course of history.[5]

History, as such, is concerned with 'what happens once'. The proper function of structural explanations for historians is to *apply* insights or models derived from generalization and abstraction. Moreover, it is such a conviction about the unique nature of historical processes which leads me to reaffirm the necessity for contingent explanations, which allow for the interlocking of different chains of cause and effect.

The role of contingency in politics is not an irritating quirk which delays or deflects events from their proper course, but a natural concomitant of the plastic complexity of the real world. It is not just that accidents will happen: causes which seem rational in retrospect may not be susceptible to prediction, because the chain of causation is unique and complex. Political leadership is a crucial link in that chain.[6]

To study this does not imply an obsession with the trivial but instead a recognition of the force of personality in unique historical situations which are no less significant for being incapable of replication. Fine books have been written about the phenomenon of revolution in the modern world; but if it is the *French* Revolution which we wish to understand, then Simon Schama is surely right to warn us against neglecting the clash of personality in explaining what actually happened: 'Overlooking these personality feuds as a serious issue in revolutionary politics has been one of the most glaring omissions of modern historiography.'[7]

*   *   *   *   *

Nowadays, of course, national leaders are highly visible and widely recognized. How far is the prominence of leadership a function of contemporary political manipulation? There was much criticism of the British General Election of 1992 as simply 'a television election'. Television did not simply report the campaign: it created the campaign, as a series of media events contrived to produce a predetermined image. This was denounced as a surrender to showbusiness, a triumph of trivia, a debasement of debate. Never in the history of electoral conflict had so much been said by so many to such little purpose. Disconsolate citizens looked in vain for the orators who once held vast crowds spellbound addressing the weighty issues of the day. 'It isn't like Gladstone, is it?', one Lancashire voter confided. 'Where has it all gone?'[8]

A glance at history shows that the Grand Old Man was actually not backward in the game of media manipulation. It was he, above all, who succeeded in using the new technology of his day to project his policy and his personality in the country. While other leaders rested on the reputation they had made in Parliament, Gladstone literally went out of doors to take politics to the people. In the process he showed that the Liberal Party could thrive amid the vulgarity attendant on a mass franchise, which horrified many of his upper-class cronies. It had no terrors for a leader manifestly able to preach a populist message.

In an age when the pulpit provided not only moral uplift but popular entertainment, Gladstone's politics of conscience were beamed at his Nonconformist followers in an idiom with which they were perfectly familiar. His charismatic presence was that of a hellfire preacher turning a providential vision into an election winner. He realized that he was a performer, playing to a public. He was a true professional who acknowledged that, whether he felt like it or not, he must 'put on the steam perforce'.[9] His steam oratory matched the steam engines which took him on his whistle-stop tours and the steam presses which produced cheap newspapers to spread the word throughout the land. Even when the train failed to stop on schedule, the presses still rolled with a verbatim account of a speech which Gladstone never made, taken down from his own dictation by the shorthand reporter from the Press Association. No soundbite was more factitious than this, only shorter. When 'the People's William' went on the stump, he was well aware that he was speaking not only to the thousands who attended his meetings but to the millions who only read about them. Professional football was catching on as a spectator sport in much the same way. The politics of vicarious participation did not have to wait for the invention of the cathode ray tube, even though poor Gladstone had to make do with newsprint to seize his opportunity – including the photo-opportunity, as shots of him felling trees sufficiently indicate.

An admirer of Gladstone's moral populism, Lloyd George developed his own distinctive style in an era when secularization had made the pulpit an obsolescent model. As A. J. P. Taylor liked to point out, Lloyd George's platform oratory owed a heavy debt to the music-hall.[10] He could control an audience with the inspired timing of a stand-up comic. His one-liner about the House of Lords – 'five hundred men, chosen accidentally from among the unemployed' – was fit to bring the house down. He was the politician as entertainer, subordinating reason to emotion as much as any recent propaganda by television. He could pirouette, like Chaplin, from the broadest belly-laugh to tear-jerking pathos. Around 1919 they were probably the two most famous individuals in the world. Yet, unlike Chaplin, Lloyd George failed to make the transition to the electronic media, and the dawn of the radio age marked his political twilight.

For Lloyd George's fans there could be only one answer to the question as to what their man did in the Great War: he won it. Just as his critics only had one answer to the question as to what he did to the Liberal Party: he ruined it. Both propositions, of course, are disputable, especially if structural explanations are preferred. It may be that the outcome of the First World War was determined by geopolitical factors which leave little scope for the impact of any British leader. But can the displacement of the Liberal Party by Labour likewise be explained in structural terms, as a simple function of the emergence of the working class? The more that these issues are explored, the more apparent it becomes that there are no longer any easy answers, if there ever were.

At one level the story is about high politics, as a game of tactical manoeuvre fuelled by personal ambition, with a constantly reshuffled pack of Ins and Outs. Here we see the slowly developing rivalry between Asquith, as the prime minister who had taken Britain into the war, and Lloyd George, the increasingly preferred candidate of those who wanted its more effective prosecution. Many Conservatives saw things this way. But so, as Jane Morgan's early work on Christopher Addison convincingly illustrated, did some politicians of irreproachably progressive outlook. It was Addison who conducted the crucial canvasses of Liberal back-bench support for Lloyd George which showed that his bid for power in 1916 could succeed.

Bonar Law's remark to Addison – 'We cannot go on like this Addison, do you think?' – raised the laconic to the lapidary: it was fit to be inscribed on Asquith's political tombstone.[11]

In the parliamentary context the great theme is the disintegration of the Liberal Party. It notoriously lost its sense of purpose and unity, especially when confronted with the conscription issue in 1915 and 1916, though it should be noted that the Conservative and Labour parties also faced new stresses, albeit ones which they ultimately proved better able to survive. The transformed position of the Labour Party in the later stages of the war can only be understood by reference to its territorial expansion throughout the country, in a process that may have been unstoppable and was certainly unstopped.

The Coupon Election of 1918 ended the long parliament which had sat throughout the war, a parliament that had been elected in December 1910 with a normal majority of over a hundred for the Liberal government. One section of this majority comprised the Irish Nationalist MPs, tied to the Liberals by the prospect of an Irish Home Rule Act to cap the series of bills which had been introduced since Gladstone's day. But by the time Home Rule was due to come into force at the conclusion of hostilities, the old Nationalist party had been swept away by an insurgent phalanx of Sinn Fein MPs who refused to take their seats at Westminster. Gone too was another pillar of Asquith's pre-war majority, for the Labour Party had now thrown off the progressive alliance with Liberalism within which it had hitherto been constrained. True, Liberal supporters of Lloyd George accounted for 127 MPs in the new House of Commons; but the majority which sustained him in power was made up with 400 Conservative (or quasi-Conservative) coalitionists (or quasi-coalitionists). Against them was a puny independent Liberal party of thirty-six MPs, which made the election of fifty-seven Labour MPs look relatively formidable.

The impressive new study by John Turner discounts any general explanation of the rise of Labour and the decline of Liberalism. With modern techniques it is possible to test a number of hypotheses about the 1918 general election. It seems to be true that the Coupon, which Lloyd George and Bonar Law jointly issued to their coalitionist supporters, succeeded in pulverizing their Asquithian and Labour opponents. This was achieved, moreover, despite the reinforced effect upon voting of class rather than religion. But Turner's analysis of the voting figures provides meagre support for the notion that the more democratic franchise introduced in 1918 was the key to Labour's advance. Indeed, rather than attributing the outcome to the new male voters, he points to the impact of women, now enfranchised if they were over thirty and in possession of a local government franchise qualification. The suggestion here is that the female franchise was associated with a class bias which at the time worked against Labour. Thus the newly enfranchised women voters swelled Lloyd George's victory. There was, Turner argues, no explosion of Labour support after the war and no general shift from a sectarian to a class base in voting patterns. 'The fragility of explanations based on class or sect is particularly striking, because it calls into question the very essence of "class" as a political concept.'[12]

The crucial factor was Labour's new-found readiness in 1918 to fight as an independent party on a broad front; and to understand this we need to understand the new political circumstances created by the war. In its course the Liberal Party was shaken apart; but it was not until November 1917, with Asquith's fitful adoption of an opposition posture, that the pre-war party system suffered irreparable damage from the war. There is little evidence of grounds for a deep-rooted schism between Asquith and Lloyd George.

In his influential account of wartime politics, Lord Beaverbrook liked to draw a contrast between Asquith, as a lackadaisical votary of *laissez-faire*, intent upon losing the war along orthodox Liberal lines, and Lloyd George, the coalitionist and conscriptionist, ready and able to deliver victory with a knockout blow.[13] This view is discounted by Turner. Instead, he argues, in 1915–16 the problem turned on the use of finite resources. All that Lloyd George's medicine would, and did, produce was a financial and economic crisis which threatened Britain's ability to wage a long war.

There are two implications to this argument. One is a coherent, if qualified, defence of the Asquith government on the grounds that it was not rational in 1916 to gamble on a quick victory – as the experience of Passchendaele subsequently proved. The other implication is that Asquith bears a heavy personal responsibility for splitting the Liberal Party during 1917–18, at a time when many of his nominal followers would have been ready to accept Lloyd George's repeated invitations to enter his administration. A twofold conclusion therefore seems appropriate. First, that the war was indeed won – eventually, expensively, unpredictably – but not simply by Lloyd George. Finally, that the Liberal Party was indeed ruined – avoidably, incrementally, irrevocably – not for reasons which were structurally determined, but through a more complex chain of causation in which leadership played an inescapable part.

*   *   *   *   *

The Churchill myth has been so potent because he was his own myth-maker. He lived out his career as a historical romance which revolved around himself. His account of his accession to supreme power in 1940 is matchless: 'I felt as if I were walking with destiny and that all my past life had been but a preparation for this hour and this trial.'[14] Here is a compelling vision of how to judge him and how to remember him, which has understandably captivated the popular imagination for half a century. But the task of history is nothing if not a critical appraisal of received versions of the past. How does the Churchillian vision withstand revisionist interpretations?

Paul Addison's is the most subtle of several recent attempts to shift our perspective. The figure at the centre of his portrait is not the great war leader of 1940 to 1945 but a substantial politician whose activities in domestic policy have often been eclipsed. Here is a man who twice crossed the floor of the House of Commons, leaving the Conservative Party for the

Liberals in 1904 and not returning until twenty years later. Here is an able and ambitious minister who burst into Asquith's cabinet as President of the Board of Trade at the age of thirty-four, who served as Home Secretary before he was forty, and who became a controversial Chancellor of the Exchequer under Baldwin for the term of a full parliament in the 1920s. Had he never gone near the Admiralty, had he retired at the age of sixty-five instead of becoming prime minister, Churchill would still have been a striking figure in British political history. He would have ranked with his friend F. E. Smith as an adventurer of glittering promise, with Aneurin Bevan as both orator and social reformer, with Enoch Powell as a wilful prophet who went into the wilderness.

It is this sense of a Churchill *not* predestined as national saviour which Addison successfully recaptures. We are given a succession of convincing pictures of Churchill at work in his chosen profession – and hard work it was, for all his immense capacity for relaxation and enjoyment. Churchill made himself into a successful orator, in the Edwardian grand manner, and gave himself something to orate about, by sheer hard graft. He learned up the fiscal question and thought Free Trade a sufficiently important issue on which to join the Liberals.

Addison notes that, contrary to many impressions, Churchill 'was captivated by ideas and longed to dramatise them on the democratic stage'.[15] In the Edwardian period it was social reform which seized his enthusiasm in this way. Not only did he pioneer the National Insurance principle as the means of dealing with cyclical unemployment, and institute a system of labour exchanges, but when he was translated to the Home Office Churchill determined to carve out a role as a prison reformer. Adopting a remarkably stark class analysis, he claimed that imprisonment was 'an evil which falls only on the sons of the working classes'. How could the law be defended when it showed such obvious partiality between classes? He braved the King's wrath in maintaining that there were 'idlers and wastrels at both ends of the social scale'. Moreover, he considered that 'every workman is well advised to join a trade union'.[16] Little wonder that Conservatives set Churchill alongside Lloyd George as a radical bogeyman in these years.

Yet this grandson of a duke was, and remained, essentially a paternalist. 'He desired in England a state of things where a benign upper class dispensed benefits to an industrious, *bien pensant*, and grateful working class', was how a Liberal colleague put it.[17] Churchill moved to the right during and after the First World War, but he did not simply relinquish or repudiate his social concerns. They were the product of a characteristic ability to make a moral and imaginative leap of sympathy across conventional boundaries of class or party. Even when he was defeated by Labour in Dundee in 1918 he commented privately: 'When one thinks of the kind of lives the poorer people of Dundee have to live, one cannot be indignant at the way they voted.'[18] If Churchill was by now on his way to rejoining the Conservative Party, he remained a maverick whose bellicosity of manner often led him to be misjudged.

Nowhere is this better shown than during the great coal dispute of 1926. Addison deftly exposes the myth of Churchill's intransigence in provoking the General Strike. But, once it had begun, Churchill's full-blooded commitment to breaking it, by all means at the government's disposal, is brought out well. After the TUC had been detached from the miners, and the miners were left isolated, Churchill emerges as the most sympathetic member of the government in trying to reach a settlement. Yet when he was frustrated in his peacemaking role, he proposed to starve out the miners and their families.

Through such episodes Churchill acquired an image as a class warrior in the eyes of the Labour movement. One achievement of Addison's book is to show how this came about. Another is to suggest how, from 1936, a faltering transformation took place, when Churchill took up the theme of resistance to Hitler. Willy nilly, Churchill emerged as the spokesman of an anti-fascist alignment with its centre of gravity on the left; and, willy nilly, the Left ultimately adopted him in this role. It is at this point that Addison's account reinforces rather than challenges traditional images. 'Churchill, on his line of march, met the

British people marching in the same direction', he writes of 1940, as the new prime minister 'suddenly found himself at the head of a column of millions of men and women drawn from all classes and parties.'[19] David Low's famous cartoon, 'All Behind You, Winston', showing him heading a phalanx of the British people rolling up their sleeves, can stand here for a thousand footnotes.

But what was it all for? 'Churchill stood for the British Empire, for British independence and for an "anti-socialist" vision of Britain' – each of them fatally compromised by 1945, according to John Charmley. He undoubtedly achieves some effective exercises in demythologization. He shows that appeasement was a process which Churchill first contested over Indian rather than European policy and that 'in both cases Churchill ignored the limitations on power'.[20] Here we approach the real red meat of the book, laid out on the slab in its coverage of the Second World War.

Does Charmley doubt that Churchill played a decisive historical role in 1940? Far from it: his point is that it was only because of Churchill, 'the essential man', that Britain stayed in the war – a war that was fundamentally unwinnable. Charmley carefully avoids saying that Britain should have opted for a negotiated peace; he simply adds to the testimony of other recent historians in showing that this was a rational option for anyone who calculated the odds in the summer of 1940.[21] Charmley's real case, which he has developed before, is that Neville Chamberlain reasonably conceived appeasement as a policy consistent with Britain's traditional objectives, and one appropriate to the country's straitened circumstances, whereas Churchill indulged in the politics of willpower.[22] The new twist is that, since willpower was not enough, Churchill had to fall back on appeasement.

There is obviously something in this. But is it just a debating point or does it point to a viable alternative course? Britain's increasing dependence on the United States is undeniable; but the real issue is how far it was avoidable. Churchill's reprimand to the proud, prickly, intractably anti-American de Gaulle –

'every morning when I wake my first thought is how I can please President Roosevelt' – may suggest that a more Gaullist attitude might have brought Britain greater dividends.[23] Yet when Churchill was overruled by Roosevelt on strategy, this simply reflected the realities of power. Perhaps Churchill's alternatives were to knuckle under with a good grace or to knuckle under with a bad grace. Likewise, Churchill's dilemma over Russian demands. How was his appeasement of Russia over the Polish border in 1944 different from Chamberlain's appeasement of Germany over the Czech border in 1938? If Churchill had no choice, perhaps he should have realized in retrospect how few options had been open to Chamberlain at Munich. But it is surely inconsistent to indict Churchill while exonerating Chamberlain.

Though, like Lloyd George before him, Churchill might have been 'the man who won the war', his achievement did not reverse the tide of national decline nor preserve the British Empire. When he promised 'victory at all costs', the ultimate costs were as uncertain as the ultimate victory. If he was walking with destiny in 1940, by 1945 he was stumbling with destiny. All this is true, and it was not wholly hidden from him. After all, he called the final volume of his war memoirs, *Triumph and Tragedy*. Yet his existential decision to fight on in 1940, his ability to impose this conviction on the British people and to mobilize their support behind his moral and imaginative vision, remains the moment in their twentieth-century history when leadership most decisively shaped the course of events. The heroic style of leadership is not synonymous with successful leadership. It does not guarantee winning the game but it certainly raises the stakes. Not only does this make politics more dramatic as a spectacle, it thereby promises to open windows of opportunity which would otherwise remain closed.

Notes

1   Eric Hobsbawm, *London Review of Books*, 23 May 1991, p.3, reviewing Peter Clarke, *A Question of Leadership: Gladstone to*

Thatcher (London, Hamish Hamilton, 1991). I am grateful to Stefan Collini, John Thompson and Maria Tippett for helping me improve this draft.

2 E. H. Carr, *What is History?* [George Macaulay Trevelyan Lectures, 1961] (London, Penguin, 1964), p. 104.

3 Ibid., p. 107.

4 For documentation of the above facts I have relied on materials in the Nagasaki Peace Museum, Japan.

5 Geoffrey Hawthorn, *Plausible Worlds* (Cambridge University Press, 1991).

6 Epilogue to Peter Clarke, *A Question of Leadership*, paperback edn. (London, Penguin, 1992), p. 332.

7 Simon Schama, *Citizens. A Chronicle of the French Revolution* (London, Penguin, 1989), p. 479.

8 Quoted in Edward Pearce, *Election Rides* (London, Faber and Faber, 1992), p. 150.

9 Quoted in H. C. G. Matthew (ed.), *The Gladstone Diaries, 1875–80*, vol. ix (Oxford, Clarendon Press, 1986), p. lxi. On the nature of Gladstone's popular appeal I am also indebted to Eugenio F. Biagini, *Liberty, Retrenchment and Reform: popular liberalism in the age of Gladstone, 1860–80* (Cambridge University Press, 1992).

10 A. J. P. Taylor, *Lloyd George: Rise and Fall*, [Leslie Stephen Lecture] (Cambridge University Press, 1961), pp. 10–11.

11 Quoted in Kenneth and Jane Morgan, *Portrait of a Progressive: the Political Career of Christopher, Viscount Addison* (Oxford University Press, 1980), p. 53. This fine book was based on the Leicester Ph.D. thesis by Jane Morgan, whose external examiner I was in 1979.

12 John Turner, *British Politics and the Great War* (Yale University Press, 1992), p. 435.

13 Lord Beaverbrook, *Politicians and the War, 1914–1916* (London, Oldbourne Press, 1959), first published 1928–30.

14 Winston S. Churchill, *The Second World War*, vol. i, *The Gathering Storm* (London, Cassell, 1948), pp. 526–7.

15 Paul Addison, *Churchill on the Home Front*, (London, Jonathan Cape, 1992), p. 128.

16 Ibid., pp. 114, 123, 146.

17 Ibid., p. 436 quoting Charles Masterman; cf. Herbert Morrison's similar comment quoted on p. 341.

18 Ibid., p. 226.

19 Ibid., p. 326.

20 John Charmley, *Churchill: the End of Glory*, (London, Hodder and Stoughton, 1993), pp. 649, 290.

21 Ibid., pp. 400, 529. There is a notably cogent and concise appraisal in David Reynolds, 'Churchill in 1940', in Robert Blake and William Roger Louis (eds.), *Churchill* (Oxford University Press, 1993), pp. 241–55.

22 See John Charmley, *Chamberlain and the Lost Peace* (London, 1989).

23 Charmley, *Churchill: the End of Glory*, p. 558.

4

Child Victims

LUCIA ZEDNER*

Researching the child victim

In the 1980s, victims shot from relative obscurity to the forefront of the criminological agenda. The decade saw the birth of national, and later local, victim surveys, of qualitative studies on the impact of crime, of victims' experiences of the criminal justice system and the need for victim services. Researchers wrote with great confidence of the ability of the victim survey to uncover the 'dark figure' of crime and so to provide a 'true' picture of the nature and extent of victimization. Hitherto, the experiences of victims had not been formally recorded and therefore were not reflected in annual returns of the official criminal statistics. The development of Victim Support, the national organization of victim support schemes, with its policy of 'outreach' work also served to draw attention to the needs of victims which had previously gone unrecognized and unmet.

Yet certain groups of victims remained largely hidden from view. Vulnerable groups such as women, the elderly, or members of ethnic minorities are less likely to make public their victimization, less likely to come to the attention of criminal justice authorities, and are less able to obtain such help as they may need in the aftermath of their offence. Of no group is this more true than children. Until Jane Morgan began research on child victims in the late 1980s, very little was known about the types of crime against them and its impact, their experiences and needs. Although some attention had been given to one specific area of crime – child sexual abuse – there was a dearth of

*The author would like to thank Anne Viney, Assistant Director, Victim Support, for her help.

knowledge about the gamut of other, often less dramatic, but not necessarily less serious, offences suffered by children every year.

It is perhaps useful to begin by relating briefly the history of Jane's research into child victimization. Victim Support had developed expertise in responding to and supporting adult victims of crime but had been extremely cautious about responding to children. Advice from the parent organization to local victim support schemes directed that they

> ... should not undertake work which is already the responsibility of a statutory social work agency or an established voluntary organization. Most cases of abuse against children will ... be referred automatically to Probation, Social Services or the NSPCC ... Cases of theft or violence against children occurring outside the family ... should only be accepted by Schemes with experienced volunteers and professional support. Parental consent should be obtained before contacting young people under the age of 17.[1]

The rationale behind this policy was clear: Victim Support wanted neither to encroach upon work already being carried out by other agencies nor did it wish to place volunteers in the position of intruding on familial relations.

In the 1980s, the organization discovered, however, that this policy left child victims of often serious physical or sexual assaults committed by offenders outside their family without any source of support. Victim Support volunteers voiced increasing concern that they were unable to help or to refer on such children.[2] More commonly still, Victim Support volunteers were observing that children who were the victims of less serious crimes or who lived in households where crimes had taken place were also in need of help. Parents also expressed concern about their children's reaction to crimes. They sought advice about the emotional impact of crime and how best to support their offspring in its aftermath. Recognizing an unmet need, but lacking sufficient information upon which to base their work, Victim Support approached the Home Office with a proposal that research should be carried out into the range and impact of crime on children. The following year, 1987, the Home Office decided to fund a two-year project on children as victims of crime and, following negotiations with the Centre for Criminological Research, University of Oxford, it was agreed that the project would be carried out by Jane and based at the Centre.[3]

The research project focused on children under the age of seventeen who were victims of crime which had been reported to the police. It set out to explore the experiences of child victims from the offence against them and its impact, through their experiences of the criminal justice process and of the response of social and welfare agencies. It examined also the policies and practices of the police, prosecution, and the courts in dealing with crimes against children. The full co-operation of the police ensured access to all recorded crimes in which children were victims in the two fieldwork areas of Oxford and Bedfordshire. In all, 884 records of crimes directly against children and 141 of crimes in which children were indirectly affected were surveyed. The latter category was included in a bid to understand something of the way in which crimes carried out against other members of the family or household may affect children. Lengthy interviews were carried out with 125 families (85 direct child victims and 40 families in which children were indirect victims) and questionnaires were filled in by a further 87. Interviews were also carried out with 250 key personnel from all the agencies inside and outside the criminal justice system who came into contact with children. And particular attention was paid to the work of Victim Support in responding to child victims both in the fieldwork areas and nationally. The study made no pretence of being a victimization survey but rather sought to examine the experience of those child victims who had come to the attention of the criminal justice system and who were therefore already some way to being recognized as victims. While this focus was largely pragmatic, it reflected also our interest in the way in which children's status as victim is constructed.[4]

Simply put, the research found that 'very few children escape the experience of victimization unaffected'[5]. The seriousness of the offence alone was no clear guide to its likely impact on any given child. A child's individual characteristics: age, maturity, personality, history, and family situation all played a part in determining the impact of the crime. This, in part, explains why two offences which have every appearance of being alike will leave one child unscathed whilst the other suffers profound and prolonged trauma. Emotional disturbance was the most common reaction of children to crime. Although those who were the direct victims of sexual or physical assault were generally more upset by the crime and exhibited the highest levels of psychological distress, many children who were victims of other, less intrusive crimes, such as theft, were also often upset in the immediate aftermath. Amongst those indirectly victimized, those whose parents had been sexually or physically assaulted suffered particularly badly, though it is notable that nearly two-thirds of those whose homes had been burgled were also upset or very upset.

Interviews with personnel in statutory, professional, and voluntary agencies coming into contact with children revealed a very low level of awareness about the effects of crime on children.[6] Almost none had considered the indirect impact on children of crimes against other members of their household. An overriding preoccupation with the sexual abuse of children appeared to have obscured recognition of the entire gamut of other crimes against children. Most worrying of all, none of the personnel interviewed considered that they had any specific responsibility to help victims other than those of sexual abuse, and few were aware that Victim Support might provide support for children.

The research project sought to present an array of new findings about child victims and their experiences of crime and the criminal justice system not only to an academic audience but to practitioners and policy-makers also. The research was presented to the Home Office at the beginning of 1990[7] and, unusually, permission was given for it to be published independently by Oxford University Press. *Child Victims: Crime, Impact and Criminal Justice* appeared two years later in 1992. It concluded: 'There should be far greater public awareness of the need of child victims, better publicity about possible sources of support, improved inter-agency co-operation, and easier accessibility for victims seeking help for themselves.'[8] And it went on to make a series of specific policy recommendations.[9] First, that all agencies dealing with children should have specific training in the identification of child victims, the effects of crime upon them, their likely needs and how help might best be given. Secondly, that the police should develop a more sensitive approach to children who are victims of all crime, not just sexual abuse, and that information should routinely be provided about the progress of the case, the availability of support and of compensation. Thirdly, for those children required to appear as witnesses in court, there should be systematic provision of separate waiting areas, derobing, and the provision of support both before and during trial. Fourthly, referral of child victims to Victim Support should be encouraged and the work of schemes with children further developed. Finally, there should be greater inter-agency co-operation between police, social workers, Victim Support, and all other professional and voluntary workers coming into contact with children in order to obviate the common occurrence of children in need 'falling through the net'.

The research findings were widely publicized and Jane was called upon to give interviews for national and local radio and press. A public presentation of the findings to the Victim Support Annual Conference in Warwick in 1990 was met with considerable interest from both scheme organizers and volunteers.[10] Significantly, Victim Support's patron, HRH The Princess Royal, later described this as 'a benchmark' in the development of the organization's policies for child victims.[11]

The remainder of this chapter will explore developments arising since, and in many cases out of, Jane's research.

It will focus on two areas in which particularly important developments have since taken place: the provision of support to child victims and the arrangements made for children called as witnesses in court.

Support for child victims

Until the late 1980s support for child victims was largely undeveloped. Whilst Victim Support was becoming increasingly aware of children in the course of its work, no one had yet developed a child-specific response. Sources of help for child victims were largely *ad hoc* and scattered among agencies with little co-ordination or provision for referral from one to another. Accordingly, and in recognition of this need, Victim Support made a specific commitment to develop policies in this area.

(i) The Bedfordshire project

In 1987 Victim Support established a 'demonstration project' on child victims to be carried out in the county of Bedfordshire. Jane was commissioned by Victim Support to monitor the work of this project alongside the larger research study. Due to initial start-up difficulties, the demonstration project continued after and built upon the findings of our own research. During this project, local police were asked to ensure that all crimes involving children were referred to Victim Support scheme co-ordinators. Volunteers were encouraged to become alert to the presence of children in the homes they visited and, following each visit, to record the effects of the crime upon them. With the aid of Jane and myself, the project worker developed a 'check-list' which was designed to enable volunteers to collect information systematically and also sought to guide them in identifying problems for which support might be needed. During the period of the project, 620 crimes involving children were identified (186 involving direct child victims and 434 affecting children indirectly).[12] This represented an increase of 50 per cent on the previous year's referrals of direct child victims and a

50 per cent increase in indirect child victims coming to the attention of volunteers. Whilst the effect of the project had clearly been to raise adults' awareness of children's needs, it was found that in three out of four cases of violence against adults, volunteers still failed to enquire after the welfare of children within the household.[13] This continuing oversight is no doubt testimony to the difficulty of approaching children or raising the issue of their welfare with parents. The apparent reluctance of volunteers to exploring explicitly the needs of children pointed to the need for further training designed to endow volunteers both with the appropriate skills and with the confidence to 'work with children'.

(ii) National training

Following the Bedfordshire project and perhaps also the recommendations made in *Child Victims*, the importance of providing support to child victims was formally recognized by the National Council of Victim Support. In June 1993 it was decided that all Victim Support volunteers should receive training about the particular effects of crime on children.[14] A special session was developed within the national training package devoted to 'children and families' to be used by both co-ordinators and freelance trainers employed by Victim Support to carry out volunteer training.[15] The session enables volunteers to identify crimes from which children suffer; to understand the concepts of 'direct' and 'indirect' victimization; to learn what is known about the impact of crime upon children; and to explore ways of helping children to overcome their fears. The training largely abandoned the traditional formal lecture approach to employ more participative techniques of group discussion and case-study analysis. This development was designed to enable volunteers to relate information based on research findings to their own experiences gained through visiting. Emphasis is laid primarily on enabling parents to help their children to recover by passing on the experience and skills gleaned from the work of Victim Support volunteers. Victim Support's approach to training can best be summarized by quoting from the address given by its Director to the organization's national conference in 1993:

> It would appear that the most effective work involves parents working closely with the Victim Support volunteer. Parents can be given help to understand their own reactions to crimes affecting their children and the ways in which these reactions might stand in the way of assisting the child. They also need to know that their children's reactions, however out of character, are probably normal ... One of the most important contributions of Victim Support can therefore be summarized as passing on experience and skills to parents to enable them to help their own children.[16]

This policy recognized the limits of what a volunteer can reasonably be expected to achieve in the normal run of a few relatively brief visits. Perhaps more important still, it reflected the sensitivity of volunteers to their position as uninvited outsiders intervening in existing family relationships. Concern to avoid in any way usurping the parental role has limited the potential for volunteers working directly with children. In general, only where parents have explicitly asked Victim Support to talk with their offspring, have volunteers supported children alone. More usually, parents and children are seen together, with the volunteer in the position of 'facilitator' encouraging the family members to talk and turn to one another for support. This strategy generally gets around the complex of ethical issues generated by the 'interference' of the volunteer in the parent–child relationship. However, if a child approaches Victim Support directly then the feeling within the organization is that it must respond to that child's request for help.

A number of these issues remain to be resolved by Victim Support: How can the child's choice whether or not to see the volunteer best be safeguarded? How should Victim Support respond where parents have declined support on behalf of the family but the child then approaches asking for help? What should the volunteer do when neither the parents nor child ask for help, but their own observations suggest to them that the child is badly traumatized and in need of professional help?

How should volunteers respond to information given to them by the child in confidence but which clearly calls for action by the family or an outside agency? These difficult questions, and no doubt others, demand careful contemplation by Victim Support if it is to avoid placing precious volunteers in an uncomfortable dilemma or exposing its own work to charges of unwarranted intrusion within the family.

The challenge facing Victim Support now, therefore, is to construct guidelines which will provide working parameters for volunteers in contact with children. These guidelines might usefully deal with how to respond to direct approaches from children, how to construct safeguards, how to deal with issues of confidentiality, and so on. Here there is much useful experience to be gleaned from the working of other organizations like NSPCC, Childline and the National Youth Agency. Victim Support has sought advice from all these bodies on how best to respond to children. Ultimately, however, the organization is loath to become another children's agency, but seeks above all to work with whole families to enable parents to provide the support their children may need in the aftermath of crime.

(iii) Victim Support work with other agencies

Despite the advances made in respect of referrals in recent years, many child victims do not come to the attention of Victim Support. It is important, therefore, that other agencies are alert to their needs. Here Victim Support also has an important role to play in raising awareness of child victims with other specialist children's agencies and with all those professionals who come into contact with children in the course of their work. Victim Support's external programme has been developed to encourage training regarding victim-awareness for other agencies in the field. Some work has been done with hospitals and, increasingly, with schools. A recent innovation is the establishment of an independent trading company intended to undertake bespoke training programmes for staff within organizations on the effects of crime. While this is a general initiative, it clearly has important potential in respect of those groups of victims like children who, as we have seen, are generally least able to make themselves and their needs known. If child victims need to be noticed by others in order to receive recognition and help, then it is vitally important that workers in all agencies coming into contact with children are alert to indications of victimization. Limited resources restrict the amount of direct training that Victim Support is able to provide but a more general project of raising victim-awareness is pursued through the news media.

(iv) Sexual assaults by 'strangers'

One of the important messages of *Child Victims* was that while there were well developed procedures for responding to children who had been sexually or physically abused within their family,[17] there was little by way of a specialist response for children whose assailant came from outside the home. Victim Support considers that inter-agency co-operation and the holding of case conferences may often be appropriate wherever the offender comes from. This is particularly likely to be the case where the offender is well known to the child and may have built up a relationship of trust over many years which is abused in much the same way as by an offender within the home. A close friend of the family, a parent's new partner, a clergyman, or local youth leader may, in practice, be in much the same relation of trust as those formally recognized as relations. Nonetheless, the official machinery of local authority care proceedings will not necessarily swing into action on evidence of abuse. Victim Support may be loath to take up the case for fear of encroaching on the territory of social services. In this grey and difficult area, children may easily 'fall through the net' and there is an urgent need for attention to be paid to the blurred distinctions between sexual abuse within the home and assaults by those not so 'strange'. Younger children probably require support from specialists trained in child abuse, but for older children in their teens there may be an argument for saying that Victim Support is as well equipped to deal with these cases as with the other sexual assault victims they currently support.

Child victim-witnesses

The second main area of change and innovation is in respect of those relatively few children called as witnesses in court. During the period of our research many important procedural and technological innovations were made in respect of child witnesses.[18] In 1988 the police and the Crown Prosecution Service were enjoined to ensure speedy progress of cases involving child witnesses and S.53 of the Criminal Justice Act 1991 provided for the by-passing of committal hearings in such cases. On the day of the court appearance itself, some judges and counsel began to remove wigs and gowns, to alter seating arrangements within the court, and to provide a microphone for the softly spoken child.

More radical modifications sought to shield the child from contact with the defendant, for example, by the introduction of screens.[19] The Criminal Justice Act 1988 introduced permission for a live video-link to allow child victims in sexual assault cases to be cross-examined without entering the court room itself. Successful and widespread use of the link led to the extension of its availability from fourteen-year-olds to seventeen-year-olds under the Criminal Justice Act 1991. Finally, and perhaps most importantly, the report of the Pigot Committee on Video Evidence (1989) recommended that in cases of alleged sexual abuse, violence or cruelty, the child's testimony should be recorded in advance of the trial and so render appearance in court unnecessary. The Criminal Justice Act 1991 took up part, but significantly not all, of Pigot's recommendations by allowing that a video recording replace the child's examination-in-chief but requiring that the child still continue to be subject to cross-examination during the trial itself (either actually in the courtroom itself or by live video-link).

While these were all important innovations, the modification of usual procedures remains, however, at the discretion of the court. The Home Office has stressed that there is no automatic right to give evidence by pre-recorded video or live television-link, nor for counsel to be introduced to the child before court, nor for judges and counsel to remove their wigs and gowns. And, as the Director of Victim Support has pointed out, 'unfortunately, most of the provisions in the UK are discretionary and evidence suggests that they are not used as often as they should be.'[20] There is perhaps a danger that expectations may be raised in the child's mind which will not ultimately be met. Given this fact and whilst warmly welcoming all these technological changes, Jane held firmly to the view that much could also usefully be done for child victim-witnesses by persons working within the criminal process.[21] The stress of giving evidence could be reduced by better liaison between police and court personnel. Inter-agency co-operation is already well-developed in respect of the investigation phase, but could profitably be extended to the trial itself. The police have a potentially important role to play in providing information about the child to the prosecutor and to the court. By co-ordination between all the agencies concerned and with advance planning, the trauma of the experience may thus be minimized. For example, where a child's first language is not English an interpreter may be needed, where the child is deaf or physically disabled special arrangements will also be necessary. The preparation of the child victim-witness, as Jane recognized, requires considerable sensitivity. Two particularly important recent innovations are the development of the *Child Witness Pack* and the establishment of the 'Child Liaison Officer' to prepare children for court and to provide support on the day of the trial itself.

(i) The Child Witness Pack
The Child Witness Pack has been developed by a consortium comprising government departments and a number of children's organizations.[22] It was developed in recognition of the increasing number of children being called to court to testify both as victims to and witnesses of crime. The pack was developed 'in the belief that children will feel more confident and be better equipped to appear at court if they understand the legal process and their role within it'.[23] Based on research and examples of good

practice from Britain and abroad, it contains a guide for parents or carers of children and two booklets for children[24] designed to familiarize them with the court system. By explaining the roles of the various people within the legal process and the purpose and meaning of the process itself, the booklets seek to build up the child's confidence in preparation for giving evidence.

The Home Office suggests that the pack should be given to all persons taking care of a child who is likely to be required to give evidence.[25] Curiously, the pack is being distributed via nominated contact points in police forces only. The rationale for this decision was that 'it was felt appropriate to have a single distribution point for carers and children linked to the criminal justice process'.[26] Although it was not intended that police officers rather than social services professionals should automatically take on the role of independent supporter for child witnesses, the decision to distribute the pack in this way is open to criticism. According the role to the police in this way assumes that they will be in contact with witnesses and their families and, indeed, that they will be in a position to know which cases are coming to trial. Since the passing over of the decision to prosecute to the Crown Prosecution Service, the police often do not have access to information about prosecution decisions and court dates. Perhaps more important still, research has shown that the police do not regard keeping victims informed as a matter of priority.[27] It does not seem likely that the police will routinely know or make the effort to know when cases involving children are coming to trial.

(ii) Child support person

The government's intention is that the *Child Witness Pack* should be used only with the assistance of an adult who is aware of the needs of child victims, knowledgeable about the workings of the criminal justice system and who has the confidence of the police and Crown Prosecution Service. There is, of course, a danger that supporting the child with the use of the pack will render the child's evidence inadmissible.

The Home Office stresses that it is important, therefore, that the supporter be 'familiar with the basic rules of evidence and the dangers of inadvertently contaminating or otherwise discrediting the child's evidence'.[28] The Home Office appears confident that there are many practitioners, both professional and voluntary, who might perform this role. In practice, it is surely questionable whether an individual who fulfils all these criteria and who is wholly independent from the case will always be readily found. At present there appears to be an *ad hoc* system for giving the role to court ushers. Victim Support has argued that its own volunteers, working as part of the 'Witness Service' in thirty-four Crown Court centres, are better placed to use the pack with children. They are specifically trained in supporting victims and have no responsibilities other than to the victim/witness. Yet this very training raises a difficulty as to how these volunteers can plausibly fulfil the dual function of supporting victims, encouraging them to talk through their experiences and express their anguish, and then also act impartially as support personnel in court. One solution adopted by Victim Support is to split the functions, with one volunteer providing support prior to trial and a second acting as a genuinely impartial source of comfort in the courtroom itself. The difficulty here, however, is funding. Such a twintrack support system would require the funding of Victim Support's Witness Service in every Crown Court. In the light of these difficulties it is interesting to note that Jane suggested another possibility: the introduction of a support person on the model of the guardian *ad litem* who would represent the child's best interest and safeguard and promote the child's welfare.[29] This has been successfully introduced in many US states and the example is one which might profitably be adopted in the British system.

(iii) The child liaison officer

Another important development is that of the position of child liaison officer established in 1992. Towards the end of that year all Crown Court centres furnished with live television-link equipment were asked to nominate a member of staff to take on the responsibility of becoming a child liaison officer. Their function would be to promote the welfare of child witnesses called to give evidence in the Crown Court and to provide a focal point for liaison with other agencies. The child liaison officer is responsible for liaising with the Crown Prosecution Service regarding arrangements for the child's attendance at court. They are also responsible for liaising with the resident judge and the listing officer to ensure, as far as possible, that any case involving a child witness progresses within the time limits laid down for each stage under the relevant Rules of Court.

Prior to the trial date, the liaison officer has responsibility for ascertaining who is to accompany the child to court, sending out information about the location of the court and, where possible, arranging for the child to enter the court buildings by a separate entrance to that used by the public. If the child so wishes, the liaison officer arranges for them to visit the court prior to the day of trial in order to familiarize themselves with the court and to demonstrate the live television-link. For the day of trial itself, they liaise with the court listing officer to ensure that the child's parent or supporter is given a reasonable time for arrival in court in order to minimize waiting, ensure that a separate waiting area is available for them, and organize toilet and lunch facilities. Where the use of the television-link is directed by the judge, the liaison officer ensures that arrangements have been made for an usher to accompany the child into the separate television-link room. As Jane rightly envisaged, it is these human rather than technological developments which offer most potential in reducing the further or 'secondary' victimization of children by the criminal justice process.

Conclusion

This brief overview records just some of the more important innovations in regard to child victims since Jane began work in this area. Jane's work was a landmark in the study of child victims and more than one reviewer recognized that the implications of her research were 'far reaching'.[30] As one who was privileged to work alongside Jane, it is gratifying to observe how many of the recommendations made in *Child Victims* are now finding their way into criminal justice policy-making. Academic researchers rarely enjoy such rapid rewards and it is testimony to Jane's rare combination of intelligence, pragmatism and vision that her work has had such an immediate and important impact.

Notes

1   Quoted in J. Morgan and L. Zedner, 'Children as Victims of Crime', paper to Victim Support National Conference (1990), pp. 3–4.
2   Social workers will generally only take up the cases of children 'at risk' from their own family.
3   The early part of the project was undertaken also by Joyce Plotnikoff. I joined the project in the summer of 1988 and continued to work with Jane until 1992. See bibliography for publications.
4   For further discussion of the methodology of the project see J. Morgan and L. Zedner, *Child Victims* (1992), pp. 41–2; and Morgan and Zedner, 'Researching child victims – some methodological difficulties', *International Review of Victimology*, (1993).
5   Op. cit., p. 182.
6   Op. cit., particularly chapter 7.
7   J. Morgan and L. Zedner, 'Children as Victims of Crime: Impact, Needs and Responses. A Report to the Home Office', (1990).
8   Morgan and Zedner, *Child Victims* (1992), p. 183.
9   Op. cit., pp. 183–8.
10 J. Morgan and L. Zedner, 'Children as Victims of Crime', paper to Victim Support National Conference (1990).
11 Address by HRH, The Princess Royal, to the 1993 National Conference of Victim Support, p. 1.
12 Helen Reeves, 'Children as Victims of Crime' – paper given at the Victim Support National Conference Warwick (1993), p. 10.
13 Ibid.
14 This is mandatory for all new volunteers from 1994.
15 Victim Support, *Basic Training Programme for Volunteer Visitors* (Victim Support, 1992), pp. 91–102.
16 Helen Reeves, 'Children as Victims of Crime' (1993), pp. 10–11.
17 For example, the procedures laid down within *Working Together* and the role of the case conference.

18 On which see the writings of J. McEwan, J. Morgan and J. Williams, J. Morgan and L. Zedner, B. Naylor, J. Spencer, and J. Temkin in the bibliography.

19 These were first introduced in a trial at the Old Bailey in 1987 and were endorsed by the Court of Appeal in the case of *R v X, Y and Z*. (1989). See J. Morgan and L. Zedner, 'The Child Victim in Court', *The Magistrate* (April 1992), p. 51.

20 Helen Reeves, 'Children as Victims of Crime', Victim Support Annual Conference (1993), p. 13.

21 J. Morgan and J. Williams, 'A Role for Support Person for Child Witnesses in Criminal Proceedings', *British Journal of Social Work*, Vol. 23 (1993), pp. 113–21.

22 These are the Home Office, the Lord Chancellor's Department, the Crown Prosecution Service, the Department of Health, Childline, The Children's Society, Children's Legal Centre, NSPCC, and the National Children's Bureau. The project was co-ordinated by Joyce Plotnikoff, University of Birmingham. The hope is that funding of the pack may be taken over by the Home Office.

23 NSPCC/Childline, *The Child Witness Pack* (1993) backcover.

24 An activity pack for younger children aged 5–9 and a conventional book for children ten years and above.

25 A letter from the Home Office, LCD, Department of Health *Child Witness Pack* (1993), p. 2.

26 Op. cit., p. 4.

27 T. Newburn and S. Merry, *Keeping in Touch: Police–Victim Communication in Two Areas*, Home Office Research Study No. 112 (1990).

28 Home Office, LCD and Department of Health 'Child Witness Pack' (1993), p. 3.

29 J. Morgan and J. Williams, 'A Role for Support Person for Child Witnesses in Criminal Proceedings', *British Journal of Social Work*, Vol. 23 (1993), 113–21.

30 Review by J. Temkin, *Legal Studies* (March 1993), p. 133.

Bibliography

Adler, Z., 'Prosecuting child sexual abuse: a challenge to the status quo', in M. Maguire, and J. Pointing (eds.), *Victims of Crime: A New Deal* (Milton Keynes, Open University Press, 1988).

Birch, D., 'The Criminal Justice Act 1991: children's evidence', *Criminal Law Review*, pp. 262–76.

Butler-Sloss, Lord Justice, 'Children in society', *Current Legal Problems* (1989), pp. 71–83.

— *Report of the Inquiry into Child Abuse in Cleveland 1987* (London, HMSO, 1988).

Chambers, G. and A. Millar, *Investigating Sexual Assault* (Edinburgh, Scottish Office, 1983).

Glaser, D. and J. R. Spencer, 'Sentencing, children's evidence and children's trauma', *Criminal Law Review*, (1990), pp. 371–82.

HMSO, *Working Together. A guide to arrangements for inter-agency co-operation for the protection of children* (London, HMSO, 1988).

Konken, G., 'The child witness – does the court abuse the child?', in G. Davies and J. Drinkwater, *The Child Witness* (1988).

Maguire, M. and C. Corbett, *The Effects of Crime and the Work of Victim Support Schemes* (Aldershot, Gower, 1987).

Maguire M. and J. Pointing (eds.), *Victims of Crime: A New Deal* (Milton Keynes, Open University Press, 1988).

Mawby, R. I., 'The victimization of juveniles: a comparative study of three areas of publicly owned housing in Sheffield', *Journal of Research in Crime and Delinquency* (1979), pp. 98–113.

McEwan, J., 'Child evidence: more proposals for reform', *Criminal Law Review* (1988), pp. 813–22.

— 'Documentary hearsay evidence – refuge for the vulnerable witness?', *Criminal Law Review* (1989), pp. 629–42.

— 'In the box or on the box? The Pigot Report and child witnesses', *Criminal Law Review* (1990), pp. 363–70.

Morgan, J., 'Children as victims', in Maguire, M. and J. Pointing (eds.), *Victims of Crime: A New Deal* (Milton Keynes, Open University Press, 1988).

— and J. Williams, 'Child witnesses and the legal process', *The Journal of Social Welfare and Family Law* No. 6 (1992), pp. 484–95.

— — 'A role for support person for child witnesses in criminal proceedings', *British Journal of Social Work* Vol. 23 (1993), pp. 113–21.

— and L. Zedner, 'Children as victims of crime: impact, needs and responses. A Report to the Home Office' (Jan. 1990).

— — 'Children as victims of crime', Paper to Victim Support National Conference (1990).

— — *Child Victims: Crime, Impact, and Criminal Justice* (OUP, 1992).

— — 'The child victim in court', *The Magistrate* (April 1992).

— — 'The Victim's Charter – a new deal for child victims?', *The Howard Journal of Criminal Justice*, (1992).

— — 'Child Victims in the Criminal Justice System' in *Offenders and Victims: Theory and Policy* edited by David P. Farrington and Sandra Walklate (London, British Society of Criminology, 1992).

— — 'Researching child victims – some methodological difficulties', *International Review of Victimology* (1993).

National Association of Victims Support Schemes *Referral Policy Document* (November 1988).
— *Confidentiality Guidelines* (November 1988).
— *The Victim in Court. Report of a Working Party* (1988).
— 'NAVSS Submission to His Honour Judge Pigot, Chairman of the Advisory Group on Admissibility of Video Recorded Interviews as Evidence in Cases of Child Abuse' (January 1989).
National Society for the Prevention of Cruelty to Children (NSPCC)/ Childline *The Child Witness Pack* (1993).
Naylor, B., 'Dealing with child sexual assault: recent developments', *British Journal of Criminology*, Vol. 29 No. 4 (Autumn 1989), pp. 395–407.
Newburn, T. and S. Merry, *Keeping in Touch: Police–Victim Communication in Two Areas*, Home Office Research Study 116 (London, HMSO, 1990).
Parton, N., *The Politics of Child Abuse* (London, Macmillan, 1985).
Pigot, His Honour Judge T., et al., *Report of the Advisory Group on Video Evidence* (London, HMSO, 1989).
Ralphs, Enid *The Victim in Court: Report of a Working Party convened by the National Association of Victim Support Schemes* (London, NAVSS, 1988).
Reeves, H., 'Victim support schemes: the UK model', *Victimology*, Vol. 10. (1985), pp. 679–86.
— 'Children as Victims of Crime' (paper given at the Victim Support National Conference Warwick 1993).
Scottish Law Commission, *Report on the Evidence of Children and Other Potentially Vulnerable Witnesses* (Edinburgh, HMSO, 1990).
Shapland, J. and D. Cohen, 'Facilities for Victims: The Role of the Police and the Courts', *Criminal Law Review* (1987), pp. 28–38.
Shapland, J., J. Willmore and P. Duff, *Victims in the Criminal Justice System* (Aldershot, Gower, 1985).
Spencer, J., 'Child witnesses and video-technology: thoughts for the Home Office', *Journal of Criminal Law* (1987), pp. 444–63.
— 'Child Witnesses, Video-Technology and the Law of Evidence', *Criminal Law Review*, (1987), pp. 76–83.
— 'Child witnesses, corroboration and expert evidence', *Criminal Law Review* (1987).
Temkin, J., 'Child sexual abuse and criminal justice – I', *New Law Journal* (1990), pp. 352–5.
— 'Child sexual abuse – 2', *New Law Journal* (March 1990), pp. 410–11.
Victim Support, *Basic Training Programme for Volunteer Visitors* (Victim Support 1992).
Williams, G., 'Videotaping children's evidence', *New Law Journal* (January 1987), pp. 108–12.

5

Race Relations in Prison: The Dynamics of Discrimination

ELAINE GENDERS and ELAINE PLAYER

This chapter is based on a paper that we delivered many times when Jane Morgan was at the Oxford Centre for Criminological Research with us, and which Jane, amongst others, urged and encouraged us to publish. It stems from research we carried out between 1984 and 1986 into race relations in prisons.[1] Since that time the Prison Department has revised and developed both its policy on race relations and the mechanisms for communicating and implementing it. However, the basic orientation and principles underlying the policy remain the same. The Woolf Inquiry into the prison riots of 1990 was, arguably, the most thorough examination of the English and Welsh prison system this century, yet it did not encompass any review of the state of race relations. The Woolf Report of 1991 did, however, propose an agenda for change which was intended to promote a prison environment which balanced the need for security and control with the requirement of justice.[2] We believe that the empirical findings of our research highlight a number of compelling issues which must be addressed if Woolf's vision of justice is to be realized for all prisoners. This chapter, after providing a general introduction dealing with the background to the research, will therefore focus on four particular but closely related issues. First, it will describe the views held by prison staff about race relations in prison and about the Prison Department's race relations policy; second, it will look at how prison officers working in multi-racial establishments develop and carry out their duties within a framework of racial stereotypes; third, it will examine the ways in which the racial stereotypes employed by prison officers are used to construct and rationalize a process of racial discrimination in prison; and finally, it will consider some of the implications of this process for the development of a just and effective race relations policy in prisons.

Background to the research

Race relations is a subject which has been notably absent from research into British prisons. One explanation is that the presence of substantial numbers of different racial groups in the prison population is a relatively recent phenomenon. It was only in June 1986 that a Home Office Statistical Bulletin was published which revealed, for the first time, the ethnic composition of the prison population for England and Wales.[3] These figures confirmed what had long been suspected by observers both inside and outside the prison system, that, in relation to their numbers in the general population, black people were substantially over-represented amongst both the remand and sentenced populations in custody.[4] The bulletin showed that although people of West Indian or African origin constituted less than 2 per cent of the general population, they represented, on 30 June 1985, 8 per cent of the 45,926 men and 12 per cent of the 1,577 women in prisons and youth custody centres (now renamed 'young offender institutions'). Other ethnic groups were less disproportionately represented. Those of Chinese, Arab or mixed origin comprised between 2 and 3 per cent of the prison population, but only about 1 per cent of the population at large. Persons of Indo-Asian origin were not over-represented at all, but formed about 2 per cent of both those in prison and in the general population. The Home Office data also made clear, however, that in comparison with White prisoners, non-White ethnic minorities were particularly over-represented amongst those remanded in custody, those serving longer sentences and those held in closed conditions. Leaving aside questions concerning the causes of these differences, this preliminary evidence undoubtedly established the significance of race for the organization and administration of the prison system.

In the United States, race relations remained largely invisible in prison studies until the 1970s, despite the fact that blacks, Mexicans and Puerto Ricans had long constituted sizeable proportions of the prison population. This so-called colour-blind approach to prison research was replaced only after the serious disturbances led by black Muslim prisoners in the 1960s and their initiation of hundreds of lawsuits, which heralded a new era of Federal involvement in prison administration. During this time there was an increasing awareness that prisoner subcultures were not simply functional adaptations to the deprivations associated with imprisonment but reflected behaviour, attitudes and beliefs which had been imported from the outside world. The influence of the civil rights movement and the growing politicization of black people in American society were seen to have spilled over into prisons. A number of important studies testified to the racial polarization of prison society and to the proliferation of distinct political organizations within the inmate culture built around racial symbolism and ideology.[5] Race relations in American prisons thus became characterized by avoidance, strain, tension and conflict. And by the mid-1970s the dominance of racial cleavages was described as the most salient feature of the prisoner subculture.[6]

The adage that what happens in America today will happen in Britain tomorrow is a fearful reminder of the importance of race relations for the prison system. This analogy cannot be taken too far, however. The development of race relations and the patterns of immigration and settlement in Britain differ in vital respects from those found in the United States. British prisons do not share the same history of racial segregation which has characterized many American institutions, and there are fundamental differences in the administration, organization and regimes of prisons in the two countries.[7] There was no evidence from the recent inquiry carried out by Lord Justice Woolf that the devastating riots in Strangeways and other British prisons in April 1990 reflected any degree of racial disharmony. But the fact that, to date, prisons in this country have not witnessed any major disorder based upon racial divisions provides no grounds for complacency. Prison society inevitably reflects, to some degree, the wider social order of which it is a part. The inner-city disturbances of the 1980s and 1990s marked growing unrest amongst black youth and, in particular, provided evidence of their disaffiliation from, and discriminatory treatment by, some of the agencies of criminal justice.

To depict the world of the prison as a microcosm of society, however, is to deny both the special characteristics of total institutions and the significance which race relations assume in this closed environment. Of crucial importance is the fundamental social divide between inmates and the supervisory staff: the hegemony of prison staff and the derogated status of prisoners characterize the structural separation of the two groups, which in terms of its absolute quality, is unsurpassed in almost all social settings in the outside community. As James B. Jacobs points out:

> It is hard to imagine a setting which would be less conducive to accommodative race relations than the prison. Its inmate population is recruited from the least successful and most unstable elements of both majority and minority racial groups. Prisoners are disproportionately representative of the more violence-prone members of society. As a result of crowding, idleness, boredom, sexual deprivation and constant surveillance prisons produce enormous inter-personal tension. [8]

Recent case law suggests that the Race Relations Act, 1976, which makes racial discrimination unlawful in the provision of goods, facilities and services to the public, does not apply to the control functions exercised by criminal justice officials acting on behalf of the Crown (*R* v. *Entry Clearance Officer ex P. Amin* [1983], 2 A.C. 818). The extent to which this exemption applies to all social, political and economic transactions within the prison has not yet been tested. However, the allocation of prison labour was subjected to judicial review in the case of Alexander (*Alexander* v. *The Home Office 1984*, 1987, E.O.R. 1987, L.R. 15, 36–7). The judgment delivered in May 1987 held that Alexander, a prisoner who claimed that he had been repeatedly refused a job in the kitchen at Parkhurst prison on the grounds that he was black, had been unlawfully discriminated against. Whilst this case represents an important landmark for prisoners' rights regarding racial discrimination, the effect of the decision is limited: since the judgment took place in a county court, it applies only to the individual case and is not binding upon other cases brought before other courts.

Nevertheless, the Home Office, as the Ministry responsible for race relations and immigration matters, has acknowledged a particular responsibility to ensure that all its constituent parts are above reproach in their adherence to the principle of equality of opportunity enshrined in the 1976 Act. Since 1981, the Prison Department has issued specific instructions to prison staff emphasizing the importance of race relations for the professionalism of the service. In 1983 a definitive race relations policy statement was issued which emphatically stated that the department was '. . . committed absolutely to a policy of racial equality and to the elimination of discrimination in all aspects of the work of the Prison Service . . .'.[9]

In 1984 the Home Office Research and Planning Unit commissioned our research. We set out with four primary purposes in mind: to chart the development, implementation and reception of the Prison Department's race relations policy; to discover the opinions and beliefs held by staff about the state of race relations in prison and to examine how they perceived their role and carried out their duties in dealing with a multi-racial inmate population; to explore what prisoners thought about race relations in prison and how inmates of different racial origins experienced imprisonment; and to identify specific aspects of prison organization and social interaction which inhibited or facilitated the effective development of the Department's policy. In designing the study, it became apparent that the scope of the subject was so wide and the issues so sensitive, that clearly defined limits would have to be set. It was agreed that the research would be confined to male prisons, and that we would carry out an in-depth study of three institutions, supplemented by data from a further nine prisons.

The three institutions included (i) a local prison, holding some 250 sentenced men, mainly for short periods of time prior to their allocation to a training prison: ethnic minorities comprised 20 per cent of the total population, most of them being of Afro-Caribbean origin; (ii) a dispersal prison holding a long-term population of about 400 inmates, amongst whom 10 per cent were ethnic minorities, spanning a wide range of racial groups, including Afro-Caribbean, African, Indo-Asian and Arabic peoples; and (iii) a youth custody centre with a population of almost 200 young offenders: between 35 per cent and 40 per cent were ethnic minorities and almost all of them were British-born. Interviews were conducted with a total of 194 prison staff, including prison governors, probation officers and teachers as well as uniformed officers; and with 158 prisoners. In addition, we consulted and gathered information from a variety of prison and prisoner records. A considerable amount of time was also spent in the establishments during the daytime and early evening, observing and participating in the routine activities of staff and inmates: from lunch breaks and playing darts to adjudications and industrial work.[10]

Race relations in prison and the Prison Department's race relations policy

It was clear from the very outset of the research that the Prison Department's race relations policy had stirred considerable controversy amongst prison staff. The uniformed officers in particular were vociferous in their criticism of officials at the Prison Service Headquarters: for 'pandering' to the 'race relations industry' and 'running scared' of the 'Race Relations Board'. One common interpretation, and indeed criticism, made by all grades of prison staff was that the introduction of a race relations policy assumed that there was a race relations problem in prisons. With a few notable exceptions, most prison staff forcefully denied that any such problem existed, at least in their own establishment, and for many, this argument was extended to the wider prison system too.

Frequently, their denial was compounded by a rejection of the idea that race relations was a relevant issue for the Prison Service. This was plainly demonstrated in the response of many prison officers to our presence within their establishment. It was not uncommon for us to be asked, for example, why we were 'wasting our time' on such research, and considerable criticism was directed at the Prison Department for wasting time, effort and money on developing a policy which was variously described as either addressing something which was not an issue, or which succeeded only in creating an issue where none previously existed. Even amongst the minority who conceded that race relations did constitute a problem in prisons, there was a discernible tendency to underplay its importance with comments such as: 'Of course we have problems here, but no worse than outside.'

Racial stereotyping

As the research progressed it became clear that there was a fundamental contradiction in the views expressed by prison staff about the significance of the racial dimension of prison life. On the one hand, there was the denial that race relations constituted any problem in prisons; whilst on the other, a majority of staff wanted to see the proportions of black inmates within individual establishments strictly controlled. This desire to limit the black population suggested that, in some aspects, at least, race was being perceived as a highly significant feature of prison life. On closer questioning, it emerged that prison staff, and in particular the uniformed officers, held in common a number of beliefs about the character and behaviour of ethnic minority inmates and about the ways in which these shaped the development of social relations. For example, it was widely asserted that different racial groups displayed distinct patterns of behaviour and responded differently to prison regimes and routines. The root causes of their criminality were also said to differ as were the nature of the problems inmates of different races experienced during the course of their sentences.

The greatest contrast was in officers' characterization of black and Asian inmates. Black prisoners were described by all but a handful of staff as arrogant, hostile to authority, estranged from the institutions of law and order, alienated from the values associated with hard work, and as 'having chips on their shoulders'. Precisely what prison officers meant by their assertion that blacks had 'chips on their shoulders' was at first unclear as the cliché appeared to encompass a multitude of sins. Nevertheless, on closer examination a common underlying theme emerged. In broad terms what they meant was that black prisoners invariably assumed an irrational sense of racial persecution and consequently felt a rancorous antipathy towards white society. More specifically black inmates were accused of 'seeing racial prejudice around every corner' and 'screaming racial discrimination at every opportunity'. Inside the prison the behaviour of black inmates was variously depicted as noisy, belligerent, lazy, demanding and unintelligent. Only six officers in the entire sample of uniformed staff did not refer to black inmates in one or more of these pejorative ways, and as many as four out of five specifically stated that black prisoners had 'a chip on their shoulder' or that they were 'anti-authority'. Sometimes these characteristics were considered to be innate and occasionally reference was made to the supposed lower position of blacks on the evolutionary scale.

Even the causes of black criminality were thought to differ from those of other racial groups. Whilst virtually no one attributed White or Asian offending to inherent anti-authority attitudes, a quarter of the officers thought that this was a major cause of offending amongst blacks. Another criticism levelled specifically against black prisoners was that although they suffered from various social disadvantages in the wider society, they nevertheless 'wanted something for nothing' and thought that 'the world owed them a living'. Officers argued that although Black inmates aspired to many of the consumerist goals of British society – setting great store, for example, upon money, expensive clothes and 'flashy cars' – they rejected the conventional means of achieving them, namely, through hard work and industry. In some instances these views were compounded by reference to the 'immigrant status' of blacks with such comments as: 'They come over here and they think that the world owes them a living.'

Black inmates were frequently perceived by prison officers as an invading force both inside and outside of the prison setting. It was not unusual, for example, for prison officers to believe that black people constituted up to a quarter of the British population. Inside the prison blacks were seen as particularly likely to band together in racially cohesive groups, which functioned to provide physical support in the event of conflict, as well as affording opportunities for the exploitation of other inmates. Such grouping was often referred to as the 'Brotherhood'. It has been noted that over half of the uniformed staff wanted to see a limit set on the proportion of black prisoners allocated to any individual establishment and, for a few, this desire was extended to include tougher immigration rules and the enforced repatriation of black people to the West Indies. In the graphic words of one senior officer: 'Look at us, we fought two World Wars to prevent Britain from becoming a German colony and now we're infested with West Indians.'

In striking contrast, Asian inmates were generally typified by staff as 'model prisoners'. Little concern was expressed about their numbers either inside prison or in the outside community. Their behaviour in prison was described as unobtrusive, hard working, polite and mutually supportive. In addition, they were credited with a high degree of intelligence, business acumen and motivation to improve their lot.

Unlike black inmates Asians were not depicted as being estranged from an acceptance of law and order, nor from the values of achievement through hard work. Their lives outside prison were thought to be characterized by highly supportive communities and closely knit families, all regulated by a strict moral code which inculcated adherence to law-abiding behaviour. Considerable respect was expressed for their cultures and religions, to such an extent that four out of ten prison officers were mystified as to why 'such strictly controlled' and 'highly religious' men had become involved in crime at all. They tended to see Asian inmates as 'one-off' offenders who were either motivated by a desire to make money in order to set up in legitimate business, or who had committed a violent crime in response to behaviour which offended against the religious and cultural order of their communities. They were not, in other words, 'regular cons'. Thus, although Asian prisoners were described as being culturally distanced from white society because they had retained many of their own customs and traditions, this was not deemed to be incompatible with the social values of British society.

Clearly, not all prison officers held these stereotypic images of black and Asian prisoners. A very small minority ascribed a strikingly different image to black inmates, characterizing them as attentive to appearance, exuberant, happy-go-lucky, easy-going and resourceful. One officer, for example, described how blacks 'take pride in their appearance – they're streetwise and good sportsmen – one thing they can do is their bird'. And, in the words of another officer, 'blacks are just naturally effusive, they enjoy life and they don't rush around – they have this easy-come easy-go attitude and I admire them for it'. Whilst for a very few prison officers Asian inmates represented all that was sly, snivelling, secretive and manipulative. What is interesting is that, regardless of which stereotypes were applied, staff were clearly focusing on precisely the same characteristics but interpreting them in either a positive or negative way. The underlying similarity, for example, between polite and snivelling, insular and secretive; easy-come, easy-go and lazy; and between noisy and exuberant can hardly escape notice.

It must be emphasized that creating ideal typical characterizations is not necessarily a prejudicial process. Most people do this as a means of interpreting and organizing their social worlds in a way that makes it easier for them to understand and respond to situations which may confront them. It is particularly functional for prison officers, whose daily work is characterized by the need to maintain control over an unwilling and unconsenting population. In this context the prison officer must always be prepared for attempts to challenge and manipulate his or her authority. Stereotyping is a means by which prison officers attempt to predict the behaviour of others in order to avoid danger or trouble and thereby maintain good order and discipline. The success of this tactic, however, depends on the extent to which the stereotypes are based upon valid generalizations, which are demonstrably helpful in achieving certain socially approved goals, or whether they are based upon unfounded and discriminatory criteria.

The existence of racial discrimination

It may be argued that attitudes are one thing and behaviour another. In other words, it might be considered acceptable, even if undesirable, for prison staff to have racist attitudes so long as they act in a professional way in their dealings at work. But we questioned whether, in practice, a person's attitudes and their behaviour are easily separated. The next and logical step, therefore, was to look for evidence of racial discrimination in prisons. This was no easy task, since there are major problems in identifying and proving the existence of racial discrimination. In the first place, it is not possible simply to rely upon gaining evidence from victims making complaints. This is because victims of discrimination are not always aware that they are being discriminated against and, even if they are aware, there is a whole range of disincentives for them to bring it to light. A further difficulty lies in actually proving that a prisoner has been discriminated against because of his race rather than because of any other legitimate or illegitimate factor.

Clearly, individual instances of racial prejudice and discrimination occur within all large organizations and the Prison Department would not claim to be an exception. However, the issue that we sought to address was not restricted to whether it was possible to identify a few individuals who were maliciously acting on their prejudices, but whether there was evidence of systemic discrimination. In other words, we sought to discover whether the ways in which the prison system itself operated fostered discriminatory practices. We looked at evidence of discrimination in four particular areas of prison life: in disciplinary proceedings; in written assessments based on inmates' records (Standard Classification Forms) about their anticipated behaviour and training needs in prison; in the process of allocating inmates to particular wings and cells; and in the allocation of work. The amount and nature of the information we managed to accumulate on each of these areas varied considerably. However, the strength of the data lies in the consistency of the findings. In all four areas the evidence pointed in a single direction – namely, toward the relative advantage of white prisoners and the relative disadvantage of black and, to a lesser extent, Asian prisoners.[11]

In the case of labour allocation, for example, there was a high level of agreement amongst inmates of all races as to what were the 'best' and the 'worst' jobs in their particular prison. The industrial workshops were by far the most unpopular form of employment due, it was claimed, to the high degree of supervision and the inevitable restrictions placed upon prisoners' mobility in this type of work. The most frequently mentioned 'best' jobs were kitchen work and being appointed as a prison 'orderly'. The popularity of these tasks emanated from the access which these jobs afforded to the 'little luxuries' of prison life. It was well known that some prisoners in orderly positions enjoyed the privilege of sitting down for a cup of coffee and a cigarette with their supervising officer, and that those who worked in the reception area of the prison were, from time to time, allowed to smoke on the job the excess tobacco or cigarettes confiscated from new receptions. Other orderly tasks were said to provide ready access to classified information regarding, for example, parole recommendations or impending transfers of prisoners. Kitchen work was rated highly by prisoners for two reasons. First, the long working hours provided a welcome break from the monotony of life on the wing. Second, there was the added attraction of being able to smuggle out items of food and, in particular, the essential ingredients of tinned fruit, sugar and yeast for brewing prison 'hooch'.

Yet in all three prisons black and Asian prisoners were under-represented in what were generally considered to be the 'best' jobs and over-represented in what were thought to be the least attractive ones. Indeed we found that some of the highly prized jobs had never been allocated to a black inmate. We looked at labour allocation at different points in time and the same pattern remained. In addition, it remained constant regardless of how long individual inmates spent in particular establishments. It would, for example, be reasonable to presume that the longer an inmate spends in one place, the greater his chances are of progressing to one of the more attractive jobs. This was patently not happening for black and Asian prisoners.

The process of racial discrimination

Senior administrators in the Prison Department would not deny that there are members within the Service who are racially prejudiced and who act on these beliefs to discriminate against particular prisoners. Indeed, we came across a number of instances where this was happening. At one of the prisons, for example, a black prisoner was sacked from his job in the kitchen on the grounds that he had stolen food from the stores. It transpired that he was caught leaving the kitchen with a small quantity of instant coffee, which was generally recognized as a routine perk for kitchen workers and had been taken advantage of by several other members of the party with impunity. At another establishment one work supervisor used a combination of tactics to 'encourage' a black inmate on his work-force to apply for another job. He frequently failed to call this man for work, leaving him locked in his cell and, when included in the party, he ensured that the least attractive jobs were allocated to him. This supervisor made no secret of his dislike of black people and told white members of his work-force that if the black prisoner did not like it, he should apply for a change of labour.

But we would argue that the evidence of racial discrimination that we unearthed was not simply the product of a few racially prejudiced individuals. This type of explanation is inadequate for three reasons. First, it fails to explain why individuals who do not share these views engage in racially discriminatory behaviour. Second, and conversely, it fails to acknowledge that individuals who hold racially prejudiced views may be inhibited or deterred from acting upon these beliefs. Although there is undoubtedly a connection between a person's attitudes and behaviour, this connection is by no means simplistic or mechanical. A number of factors, such as explicit social norms or severe legal sanctions, may intervene to militate against putting these prejudicial beliefs into practice. And third, explanations which rest upon individual racial prejudice alone fail to explain why institutions behave consistently over time despite changes in personnel.

We would suggest that racial discrimination was, at the time of our research, intrinsic to the social organization of prisons. Furthermore, we believe that despite efforts by the Prison Service to inculcate professional standards of conduct, racial discrimination is likely to persist because the prerequisites for its existence remain very much a part of prison life. It is the consequence of a complex interaction between racial stereotyping, on the one hand, and, on the other, the attempts by prison staff to achieve the multifarious and sometimes conflicting goals of the establishment. Most importantly it is a process which is not unique to prisons. Valerie Karn, for example, describes how it operates in the allocation of housing.[12] She has shown how, at times of scarce resources, building societies and local authorities are unable to meet all of their objectives and have to give priority to some over others. Karn argues that in ordering their priorities racial stereotypes are used, which systematically produce advantages for white applicants over ethnic minorities.

Prisons, too, have a number of competing organizational goals. These include the need to provide treatment and training; to keep prisoners in secure custody; to maintain good order and discipline; to treat prisoners humanely and with respect in accordance with the Prison Rules; and to ensure equality of treatment to all prisoners regardless of their race. It is obvious that, in certain circumstances, these aims can be perceived as being in conflict. For example, when there are severe staff shortages, the continuance of treatment and training programmes may be regarded as jeopardizing custodial security. When this sort of conflict arises, staff are required to establish their priorities and adjust their behaviour to achieve certain goals rather than others. We would argue that when prison officers prioritize their goals they draw upon racial stereotypes which systematically rationalize a certain kind of outcome: namely, the relative advantage of white prisoners and the relative disadvantage of ethnic minorities. In essence what happens is that prison staff emphasize the goals of good order and discipline, together with management objectives associated with the efficient running of their establishments, at the expense of those goals which are concerned directly with prisoners' treatment and welfare. The following two examples serve to illustrate how this process can work.

Example one.   At one establishment it emerged that over the past two years there had never been a black inmate appointed to the prized post of receptions orderly. This was a job which required the prisoner to work closely with a small number of staff who were responsible for processing prisoners and their property when first received into the establishment, or when being discharged or transferred to other prisons. There was no evidence to suggest that the officers who had been responsible for this appointment held hostile attitudes towards blacks. Repeatedly it was stated that staff chose 'the best man for the job' irrespective of race. It then became apparent that a conflict of organizational goals existed between, on the one hand, ensuring equality of opportunity for all inmates regardless of race and, on the other, the need to appoint the 'best man for the job' in order to achieve organizational efficiency. In this case staff gave priority to the latter goal and drew upon racial stereotypes to justify the non-employment of black prisoners. Officers argued that it was a job which ideally required somebody who was a 'loner'; someone who could be trusted with confidential information and access to restricted property, such as money and tobacco; and someone who would not be confronted with torn loyalties if asked by other inmates to smuggle contraband through from reception. Given these criteria, staff argued, it was hardly surprising that there had been a lack of black inmates appointed, because black prisoners hardly ever fell into the category of a 'loner': they were nearly always part of a group and their loyalty to the black group overrode any other responsibility.[13]

Example two. At two of the three establishments staff routinely dispersed black prisoners across and within wings to ensure that the proportion of black inmates on any individual spur or unit did not exceed a certain limit. Their justification for this was that, typically, black prisoners grouped together and sought to dominate wings; that white prisoners were intimidated by the presence of black inmates in large numbers; and that inter-racial power struggles would inevitably break out unless the proportion of black prisoners was controlled. Again, there was an evident conflict of organizational goals, this time between ensuring equality of treatment to all inmates and maintaining order on the wings. And again, staff gave priority to the latter goal. Prison officers tended to empathize with the feelings they projected onto the white prisoners, perceiving blacks as an invading force. In consequence, these beliefs led staff to take account of race when they were assigning accommodation to blacks but not when they were assigning accommodation to whites.

Implications for the development of a race relations policy in prisons

A frontline defence of racial discrimination in prisons is the argument that prisons simply reflect what is going on in society at large. In other words, it is inevitable, even if undesirable, for there to be racial prejudice and racial discrimination in prisons because that is precisely what is happening in the outside world. There is obviously some truth in this proposition, but there is also the danger that it can lead to an oversimplification of the problem. To depict the social world of the prison simply as a microcosm of society is to deny the special characteristics of prisons and to overlook the consequences which these have for race relations. By way of illustration, we would argue that there are three features of the occupational culture of prison officers which represent a fundamental dilemma for the development of a race relations policy in prisons.

First, the intrinsic conditions of a prison officer's work actually encourage, and indeed rely upon, stereotyping. This, of course, is not limited to racial stereotypes but includes the stereotyping of a wide range of inmate groups, such as terrorist prisoners, sex offenders and young offenders. One of the reasons that stereotyping has become particularly functional for prison officers is that their work has been characterized within the occupational culture by three interdependent features: authority, suspicion and danger. These features are drummed into them throughout their training: they are the men in authority and their authority must be maintained in all situations; they must be constantly watchful and suspicious because they are dealing with a population who will take any opportunity to challenge their authority; and thus, they are constantly in a situation of potential danger. Within this context, stereotyping can be seen as an attempt by prison officers to predict the behaviour of others in order to achieve their goal of maintaining good order and discipline.

Second, racial stereotyping is not only encouraged by the ways in which a prison officer's role is defined, it is also reinforced by the social context in which he lives and works. It is a milieu characterized by conditions which inevitably create a degree of social isolation and internal solidarity. Shift work and the problem of 'switching off' from the highly charged atmosphere of the job create a situation in which much off-duty socializing occurs with others who work in the Prison Service. The opportunity to move anywhere in the country during the course of their career and the probability of transfer following promotion also contribute to their dependence upon the Prison Service for their social contacts. These pressures towards in-group socializing are further reinforced by the provision of staff clubs attached to each prison, encouraging officers and their families to mix socially. Since very few prison officers are members of ethnic minority groups, social relations with black and Asian people are predominently focused upon their interactions with inmates.

Internal solidarity is closely linked with the social isolation of officers but it is also a product of the intrinsic conditions of the job and the consequent need to be able to rely on colleagues in a tight spot. Inevitably a 'them and us' outlook develops which creates its own internal pressures for the identification of conformity amongst fellow officers. As in every large organiza-tion, inter-personal conflicts exist but these detract little from the powerful internal solidarity characteristic of the officer subculture. In addition, prison officers appear to be an extremely homogeneous group. A study carried out by the Office of Population Censuses and Surveys revealed that, in general, they appear to be drawn from the most conservative sectors of society. At a time when a military background is becoming increasingly rare, as many as half of all prison officers had served in the armed forces, most having been volunteer regulars and not National Servicemen.[14] It was suggested that many had been attracted to the Prison Service because it is a highly disciplined and hierarchical organization which provides the security and well-ordered working environment that civilian life does not.

The third and final area of the occupational culture which we believe has implications for the development of a race relations policy in prisons is the officer's sense of professionalism. This has a bearing not upon stereotyping but upon the ways in which priority and importance are attached to certain organizational goals over others. During our fieldwork, a considerable degree of discontent was expressed by prison officers about what they considered to be the absence of any 'end product' to their work. They felt that the only function of imprisonment was that of containment and that their role had been relegated to that of custodian. As a result, their sense of professionalism was closely bound up with the pride they could take in the smooth running of their own establishment. Goals associated with management and control, which assisted the organizational efficiency of the institution, consequently became elevated to paramount importance at the expense of other types of goals and, in particular, at the expense of the goal of racial equality. Moreover, the prison officer's sense of professionalism also plays an important part in the denial that race relations is either a problem or an issue in prisons. Clearly, if their professionalism is seen to be tied up with the smooth running of their establishment then there is considerable pressure to play down difficulties and to define as problems only those issues which seriously threaten their primary goal: the management and control of the establishment. The Woolf Report has unambiguously stated that the objectives of security and control must be balanced against the requirements of humanity and justice. The government has similarly acknowledged the fundamental wisdom of this message.[15] Its achievement hinges critically upon a recognition that race relations have an important role to play in establishing managerial priorities and in informing operational evaluations.

Notes

1 The research was carried out at the University of Oxford Centre for Criminological Research. It was commissioned and funded by the Home Office Research and Planning Unit.

2 Lord Justice Woolf, *Prison Disturbances April 1990: Report of an Inquiry by the Rt. Hon. Lord Justice Woolf (parts I and II) and His Hon. Judge Stephen Tumin (part II)* (London, HMSO, Cmd 1456, 1991).

3 Home Office, *The Ethnic Origin of Prisoners: The Prison Population on 30 June 1985 and Persons Received July 1984–March 1985*, Statistical Bulletin (1986).

4 The research was concerned with prisoners who fall within three broad racial categories: those of Caucasian descent, those of Afro-Caribbean descent, and those of Indo-Asian descent. Throughout the

paper these groups are referred to as 'whites', 'blacks', and 'Asians', respectively. This reflects the terminology which was employed by both prison staff and prisoners to describe and distinguish between the three different racial groups.

5   See T. Davidson, *Chicago Prisoners: the Key to San Quentin* (New York, Rinehart and Winston, 1974); J. Irwin, *The Felon* (Englewood Cliffs, N.J., Prentice Hall, 1970) and also 'The changing social structure of the man's prison', in D. Greenberg (ed.), *Corrections and Punishment* (Beverley Hills, Calif., Sage Publications, 1977); L. Carroll, 'Race Ethnicity and the Social Order of the Prison', in R. Johnson and H. Toch (eds.), *The Pains of Imprisonment* (London, Sage, 1982).

6   J. Irwin, *The Felon.*

7   See H. E. Barnes and N. K. Teeters, *New Horizons in Criminology* (Englewood Cliffs, N.J., Prentice Hall, 1959).

8   J. B. Jacobs, 'Race relations and the prisoner subculture' in N. Morris and M. Tonry (eds.), *Crime and Justice: An Annual Review of Research* (Chicago University Press, 1979), p.23.

9   Prison Department Circular Instruction 56/1983, Home Office (1983).

10 For a full account of the methodology see E. Genders and E. Player, *Race Relations in Prisons* (Oxford, Clarendon Press, 1989).

11 For full details of the empirical findings see E. Genders and E. Player, op.cit.

12 V. Karn, 'Race and housing in Britain: the role of the major institutions', in N. Glazier and K. Young (eds.), *Ethnic Pluralism and Public Policy* (London, Heinemann, 1983).

13 There was no evidence from the research that black inmates were any more likely than white inmates to form racially cohesive groups. Interviews with inmates designed to explore their friendship patterns revealed that white inmates were more likely than black inmates to name only others of the same race amongst their friends both inside and outside the prison.

14 Office of Population Censuses and Surveys, *Staff Attitudes in the Prison Service* (London, HMSO, 1985).

15 Home Office, *Custody, Care and Justice: The Way Ahead for the Prison Service in England and Wales* (London, HMSO, Cmd 1647, 1991).

6

Justice and Responsibility in Prisons

ROD MORGAN

There is abundant evidence as to the social marginality of prisoners prior to their incarceration. Yet few observers find it easy to see prisoners as victims. Prisoners may disproportionately have experienced local authority care as children. Few of them may have educational qualifications of any kind. A significant number may be mentally disordered. Most may have been unemployed prior to their incarceration. And a good many may have been homeless before they were allocated a cell to live in.[1] Nevertheless, the prisoners about whom the public know most – those whose criminal exploits have been widely reported by the media – tend to have committed acts too dreadful for most commentators to make the moral leap required in order to see them as victims. The miseries of those who have suffered at serious offenders' hands are all too palpable for us generally to have much sympathy with their aggressors when later they become prisoners: to do so we would have to engage with the complexities of relative social disadvantage and state power, the uncertain terrain of disrupted childhoods and the ambiguities of psychiatric diagnoses. Even if we acknowledge that only a small proportion of those offenders who experience imprisonment have committed morally outrageous acts – approximately two-thirds of all those sentenced to imprisonment are guilty of property offences not involving violence[2] – their eligibility for victim status is for most people too tenuous to be credible. It is all too easy to agree with the tabloid press's frequently intoned conclusion: just deserts – most poor or disadvantaged people do not commit serious crimes, certainly not repeatedly; if prisoners do not like the conditions of their confinement, let them take care to stay out.

For the same reasons it is difficult to think of prisoners as persons worthy of respect or capable of fulfilling duties. Are they not, by definition, the most irresponsible of our fellow citizens? Thus, to the extent that prisoners are denied the opportunity to make choices, is that not the essence of their punishment, the just outcome of their behaviour? Do not prisoners forfeit the right to be considered responsible because they have so conspicuously demonstrated that they are not?

The purpose of this essay is to question the logic and social utility of these assumptions and to argue for contrary propositions. Responsibility and imprisonment *are* uncomfortable bedfellows. But they are not incompatible. They can co-exist within limits. Moreover, a theory of imprisonment not grounded on the concept of the responsible prisoner runs the risk of contravening principles of justice and humanity. My starting point is the proposition, almost universally agreed, that no one should be subject to the sanction of imprisonment whose responsibility for their behaviour – their guilt – is in doubt. I shall extend this principle and argue that prisoners should retain all those rights inherent in the status of citizen that are not expressly taken away by Parliament. Further, that prison administrators should maximize the degree to which prisoners are made responsible for their lives both within and without prison.

I shall also presume the converse of the propositions outlined above. Namely, that treating prisoners as not responsible contravenes the basic tenets of our criminal justice system. It turns prisoners into sacrificial objects instead of being subjects of justice. They thus become victims. And to the extent that imprisonment denies prisoners' moral agency and human potential, it serves only to alienate them from the society of responsible citizenship. They thus become true outsiders. In the long run this can only increase the likelihood that we who exclude them will in turn become their victims.

The purpose of imprisonment

During the 1980s it became fashionable, particularly among penal administrators, to avoid the question of the purpose of imprisonment. This is not surprising. The only Royal Commission in English constitutional history never to have produced a report was that on the Penal System in 1964. After two years of deliberation, the committee went back to the Home Secretary to tell him that they had not reached first base. Since they could not agree on the purpose of the penal system, there seemed little point in debating its mechanics. The Commission was abandoned. Thus in the 1970s and 1980s, partly as a consequence of such unresolved debates, it became commonplace to bypass basic questions of purpose. This tendency was exacerbated when the noble purposes of 'treatment and training' which had informed the legal framework within which the Prison Department operated, and broadly guided the operational administration of the system ever since the Second World War, was first questioned and then effectively abandoned. Critics claimed that the 'treatment and training' leading to a 'a good and useful life' referred to in Prison Rule 1, was a rhetorical doctrine that had never squared with the reality of prison life. It was too vague a formulation ever to be operationalized and in any case it pretended to an expertise that staff did not possess.[3] There was little evidence that neither the different prison regimes nor the several 'treatment' programmes that had been developed made any significant difference to the reconviction rates of released prisoners,[4] in which case the authoritarianism or paternalism which characterized a system in which staff made decisions about what was good *for* prisoners was without justification.[5] Justice, it was ironically pointed out, in several respects stopped at the prison gates.[6]

Yet the 'back to justice' movement made little headway in the 1970s and 1980s, at least as far as British prisons were concerned. It was agreed 'that the rhetoric of "treatment and training" [had] had its day' but the rival formulation of 'human containment' was thought to be insufficient, 'a means without an end . . . a moral vacuum' which might turn prisons into 'human warehouses'.[7] The regrettable result was that the vacuum left by the decline of the rehabilitative ethic was filled by a preoccupation with security, the ill-resourced system was over-loaded with prisoners and the Prison Department drifted without a framework providing for prisoners' rights into the managment of 'inhumane warehouses'. There was truly a moral vacuum. The Prison Act 1952 and the Prison Rules 1964 remained (as they still do)[8] while senior management, more in accordance with the requirements of the government's financial management initiative[9] than any new sense of purpose, agreed a Statement of Tasks which was all about technical means in pursuit of undeclared philosophical ends. To say that the system was 'to use with maximum efficiency the resources of staff, money, building and plant made available . . . in order to fulfil . . . the relevant provisions of law',[10] was to say little when all that the law required was pedestrianly technical: delivering the untried and unsentenced to court; keeping everyone in secure custody; providing prisoners with 'as full a life as is consistent with the facts of custody, in particular . . . the necessities of life'.

This formula did not suffice. Despite the best efforts of some senior administrators working on aspects of operational policy (see, for example, the report of the Control Review Committee on long-term prisoners, Home Office, 1984) the prison service drifted into a managerialist era lacking clear leadership and without what one member of the Prisons Board termed a 'Sense of Direction'.[11] Morale suffered and, not surprisingly, trouble flared. The system was wracked by almost continuous industrial unrest and perennial prisoner disturbances. But in April 1990 a catalytic event occurred. There erupted at Strangeways Prison, Manchester, the longest and most serious riot in English penal history. It continued for three and a half weeks. Each night millions of television viewers watched the banners of protest and theatrical confrontational gestures of those prisoners who held out on the roof. While they remained there, their example was followed by prisoners in a score of other prisons. The scale of destruction and the political embarrassment were too great for the usual internal inquiry to suffice. The Home Secretary appointed a judicial inquiry under Lord Justice Woolf. Within a year Woolf produced a report which went well beyond the expected account of what had happened.[12] His 600-page report was hailed as the most searching analysis of prisons policy to be produced since the Gladstone Report, which had heralded the principle of prisoner reformation in 1895. Whatever the fate of Woolf's recommendations, his report is certain to set the agenda for prison reform well into the twenty-first century. At the centre of his thinking was the concept of justice.

The Woolf formula

At first glance the Woolf Report is disappointingly thin when it comes to a discussion of the purposes of imprisonment. No history of the debate is provided and there is no radical critique of the Prison Service's current Statement of Purpose. However, Woolf's brief criticism of existing formulations – the absence of any reference to justice and the failure to provide specifically for unconvicted prisoners – unlocked a process of logic with radical implications.

In Woolf's view, the orderliness of prison communities depends on three organizational principles – security, control and justice – being kept in balance. The first two ingredients have been much discussed and are well understood. Security refers to the discharge of the Prison Services's first responsibility – making sure that those suspects and offenders committed by the courts to prison stay there. Control refers to the safety of prisoners and personnel within prison, though unlike security it is the means rather than the end. Order is the objective, control the means: many controls arguably subvert order. Justice – Woolf's principal contribution to the debate – was given several meanings by him. Most important, perhaps, was Woolf's linkage between the objectives pursued by sentencers when punishing offenders with imprisonment and the purposes of those who administer prisons – very different, though ideally congruent, issues.

Woolf argues that when the Prison Service talks about serving the public it should do so by more than simply keeping people in custody. The Prison Service will serve the public best by furthering the objectives of the criminal justice system generally, namely, by preventing crime. And that objective, he claims, will best be pursued by: looking after prisoners with humanity; safeguarding prisoners' civil rights that have not been taken away by Parliament either expressly or by necessary implication; minimizing the negative effects of the experience of imprisonment; requiring 'the offender to confront and take responsibility for the wrong-doing which resulted in his . . . imprisonment'; providing the 'prisoner with an opportunity to obtain skills which will make it easier to obtain and keep employment and enable him to maintain his family and community contacts'; ensuring 'that life in prisons . . . [is] as close to life outside as the demands of imprisonment permit'; and by seeing 'that the prisoner is properly prepared for his return to society'.[13] None of this should be taken to mean that Woolf favours a return to the 'treatment' model. On the contrary, he categorically asserts that imprisonment is not justified for reformative purposes, nor is 'being a criminal . . . a creative condition'.[14] Nevertheless, it is the Prison Service's duty to ensure that the experience of imprisonment is as positive as it can be made, and to the extent that prisoners leave prison embittered or alienated then a disservice will have been done to the broader purposes of crime prevention.

> If the Prison Service contains [the] prisoner in conditions which are inhumane or degrading . . . then a punishment of imprisonment which was justly imposed will result in injustice . . . it is the Prison Service's duty to look after prisoners with humanity. If it fulfils this duty, the Prison Service is partly achieving what the Court must be taken to have intended when it passed a sentence of imprisonment.[15]

Woolf is arguing that Alexander Paterson's famous dictum – that offenders are sent to prison '*as* a punishment, not *for* punishment'[16] be taken seriously. Or, to take a more recent formulation, that 'imprisonment itself . . . is the punishment inflicted by law and no further available hardship should be imposed on a prisoner except by way of formal disciplinary action'.[17] Further, he is implicitly arguing that what I have elsewhere described as the 'new realism' in sentencing philosophy[18] – namely, scepticism regarding the individually deterrent impact of custody, disavowing that imprisonment is ever justified on purely rehabilitative grounds, and reserving the use of custody for only those occasions when the seriousness of the offence requires the denunciation of imprisonment or its use for public protection – is consistent with what we may term a neo-rehabilitative rights-based approach to the management of prisons. The state has a duty to *facilitate* rather than *coerce* rehabilitation.[19] Within this model the state should not assume that it knows what is best for the prisoner and give him 'privileges' at the discretion of management. On the contrary, the approach:

> . . . emphasises the view that the legal rights that prisoners retain as citizens generate feelings of dignity and self-worth, that prisoners are legally responsible individuals and must be treated accordingly, that the state has a duty to ensure that prisons are not destructive environments, and that potentially self-improving facilities and programmes are not provided at the discretion of the administration to be downgraded whenever it is administratively convenient or judged ineffective.[20]

Woolf's operational recommendations are based on the proposition that security, control and justice have not been balanced. Security has been over-emphasized (he recommends, for example, that remand prisoners be subject to less security than is currently required unless there is evidence that higher security status is necessary), justice has been under-emphasized (for example, prisoners have typically not been given reasons for decisions such as transfers and security categorizations which have a critical bearing on their quality of life) and inappropriate control measures have been applied (for example, those prisoners preyed on, rather than their aggressors, have often been subject to impoverished segregation). Disorder has been the consequence, most disastrously at Manchester in April 1990. Indeed, it is possible to discern from Woolf's diagnosis a process which a sociologist might term a disorder amplification spiral. The injustice of life in many prisons – the intolerable conditions repeatedly described by successive Chief Inspectors of Prisons[21] and the unaccountability of many decisions – have served to alienate and embitter prisoners in precisely the way that Woolf deprecates. Prisoners have protested in various ways. The resulting disorder has made both staff and prisoners feel insecure. The insecurity of prisoners has served to bolster the power of the strong and make even more vulnerable the weak; the prisoner subculture which is typically dominated by career criminals has been strengthened. Similar processes have been at work on the staff side; the traditional prison officer culture has survived and progressive initiatives have been marginalized. Official 'control and restraint' techniques and 'underground' sanctions have prevailed; there has been too little trust and negotiation. Justice has been further undermined. Disorder has become frequent and security has been threatened.

Woolf's many recommendations are designed to reverse this tendency. There should be a network of 'contracts' or 'compacts' to govern relationships at all levels of the Service – between the Secretary of State and the Director General, between headquarters and governors, between governors and officers, and between prisoners and local managers. The reasoning is that there is 'a "major geological fault" in the prison landscape . . . [namely] the unpredictable and volatile size of the prison population',[22] and this unpredictability destabilizes relationships throughout the system right down to the critical relationship between the prisoner and the prison officer on the cell-block landing. Thus, in the same way that the contract between the Home Secretary and the Director General should set out the tasks and objectives for the Service for the coming year alongside a statement of resources, so a prisoner allocated to a particular prison should be able to know fairly precisely what his entitlements are in terms of the daily routine and access to facilities and programmes. In the case of prisoners this could lead to the generation of 'legitimate expectations' which 'could provide a platform for an application for judicial review' were those expectations unreasonably not met.[23] Over time, prisoner contracts should lead to the promulgation of a set of aspirational standards, to a system of accrediting prisons for having achieved those standards and, eventually, to the incorporation of those standards in a new set of much more specific Prison Rules.

There is not space here to describe all the ingredients in the Woolf package, but one proposal – that 'community prisons' be developed – is important for the discussion of prisoner responsibility that follows. The doctrine of treatment and training has involved the specialization of establishments and a process of prisoner allocation to them. Prisons are either 'local' prisons, whose function is largely to serve the courts, or 'training' prisons to which sentenced prisoners are allocated after being assessed at the local prisons. Local prisons are well known to the public at large. They are almost entirely large old Victorian, radial establishments in the centres of our major cities and county towns – Leeds, Liverpool, Brixton, Birmingham, Swansea, Dorchester, Exeter and so on. Moreover, as the prison system became progressively more overcrowded in the post-war period, the local prisons became under-resourced squalid sinks in which little positive was attempted. Overcrowding was concentrated in the local prisons as a matter of policy because the noble mission of treatment and training was being carried on in the training prisons, an increasing proportion of which were new purpose-built establishments on green-field sites, and because the majority of prisoners in the local prison – the untried and short-term sentenced – were either ineligible for treatment or training or in prison for too short a time to make the attempt worthwhile. It was thought sensible to protect the new training prison jewels in the treatment and training crown.

Woolf's concept of the 'community prison' calls much of this framework into question. He points out that the majority of prisoners, including the vast majority of those received under sentence, are in prison for days, weeks or months, not years. He stresses the importance of prisoners maintaining their community ties, or of community ties being fostered when they are lacking. These efforts – particularly through more generous visiting allowances in better-quality surroundings – will best succeed if prisoners are generally held in establishments physically proximate to their community ties and if those establishments have more permeable walls, that is to say, if the various agencies with whom prisoners have dealt prior to their incarceration and with whom they will have to deal again on their release are more actively involved within the prison. These 'community prisons' should become the norm, with only a minority of long-term and special-needs prisoners being allocated to high security and other specialized establishments serving regional or national functions. This suggests that the number of local or community prisons should be greatly increased. In those parts of the country generating few committals, community prisons should be multi-functional establishments in which different categories of prisoners – men and women, young and old, untried, unsentenced and sentenced – might be held in separate small units. In metropolitan areas, community prisons might comprise local clusters of more specialized establishments.

Prisoner responsibility

Though there are references, as we have seen, to the idea of prisoner responsibility in the Woolf Report, the idea is not specifically developed. Rather it is implicit. In what follows I shall attempt to develop the idea.

The first point to make is that personal responsibility is central to the concept of legal guilt within the criminal justice system. If follows that no one should be subject to a sentence of imprisonment unless the court is satisfied that they were culpably responsible for whatever offence they committed. If, for example, the harm was serious and they were so mentally ill that they were not responsible, they should be in a hospital. When a prisoner is released from prison we expect him or her to lead a law-abiding life: the crime has allegedly been paid for. The fact that the majority of prisoners do not lead law-abiding lives on release – approximately half of all adults and two-thirds of all young adults are reconvicted within two years[24] – probably tells us as much about their reduced life chances as a result of imprisonment as it does about their essential character. Two questions arise from these disturbing data. First, was any attempt made during their period of imprisonment to get these offenders to face up to their offending behaviour? Second, since it is widely acknowledged that serious recidivism is closely associated with offenders' declining stakes in conformity, was everything compatible with the fact of custody done whilst the offenders were in prison to enhance their stake in conformity? No great discussion is needed in order to come rapidly to the conclusion that the answer to both questions has almost universally been negative. It has been commonplace for offenders to report that during the months that they languished in prison no one saw it as their business to discuss with them their pattern of offending. Further, the prison system historically has done more to frustrate rather than encourage familial and other relationships. For many years telephones were not introduced, many visiting rooms were humiliating environments within which to try to maintain relationships through infrequent visits, letters were restrictd and routinely censored without care for the sensitivities of correspondents, home leaves were few and conjugal visits forbidden.

When Woolf recommends that prisoners be required to confront and take responsibility for their offences he is advocating a programme which, somewhat surprisingly, is currently applied to only a minority of prisoners. At Grendon Underwood, Britain's only therapeutically oriented prison to which prisoners may temporarily be transferred as volunteers, the regime is geared to participation in group discussion in which offending behaviour is the primary focus.[25] During the last year or two a cognitive-behavioural programme has been systematically introduced in designated centres to which all prisoners convicted of sex offences serving sentences of four years or more have been allocated. These are exceptions, however. Most prisoners are not required to take any more responsibility for their offences than their own consciences dictate. Indeed, the harsh realities of prison life encourage, as the Prison Reform Trust in a damning account of the largely segregated arrangements for sex offenders recently pointed out, irresponsible fantasies about past and future offending to flourish.[26]

Woolf's recommendations that the number and quality of contacts between prisoners and their families be increased have already received an encouraging response from the government: the minimum allowance of visits and home leaves has been increased.[27] The improvement is justified by the observation that criminal careers are most likely to come to an end to the extent that offenders have responsibilities and ties likely to be prejudiced by their offending behaviour. Further, it acknowledges the fact that though prisoners may by definition have behaved irresponsibly, this does not mean that they are not capable of behaving responsibly nor that they cease to have responsibilities. They remain fathers or sons, mothers or daughters, husbands, wives or partners, neighbours, house-holders, employees or employers. In most respects, as has often been pointed out, it is tougher and more of a punishment to be the partner of a prisoner struggling to keep a household and family together in straightened financial circumstances, than it is to do time as a guest of Her Majesty in an establishment where everything is found. Part of the idea of the community prison is that prisoners be encouraged to face up to the community responsibilities which they face up to and which, in most cases, they will shortly be expected to take on in full again.

Prisoner responsibility goes further than the maintenance of responsibilities in the community, however. Prisons have traditionally infantilized prisoners, rendered them powerless, taken away all responsibility for day-to-day decision-making.

Part of Irving Goffman's seminal discussion of 'total institutions'[28] was his description of the way inmates are subjected to total control and subordinated to an encompassing regimen by the institutional authorities. Nowhere was this truer than in prisons. Prisoners were robbed of choice. Everything was done by the clock. Everything was communally provided. Everything personal was taken away. This is less so today than once it was, but in Britain the tradition of communal provision and lack of choice has been highly resistant to change. Only now are prisoners beginning in some establishments to be allowed to provide, wear and launder their own clothes, or choose and cook their own food. Only recently have new prisons, let alone the refurbishment programme for old ones, provided electric sockets and lavatories in single cells so that prisoners can enjoy a modicum of privacy and control over how they spend their free time. Meanwhile, the debate about the exercise of more fundamental prisoner responsibility has only just begun. Two examples will suffice to illustrate the issue.

Woolf's proposals regarding community prisons pose fundamental dilemmas to which the government has correctly drawn attention. There are competing aims that 'may be irreconcilable'. The greater the degree to which prisons are specialized, or different categories of prisoners are required to be separated from each other, or prisoners have to be held within a prison which caters exclusively for a particular committal area, the less likely is it that the prison estate will be used efficiently and overcrowding will be avoided. Thus, because the prison estate is not well matched with the geographical distribution of committals, is it preferable that young offenders or unconvicted prisoners on remand should be held in less crowded conditions with prisoners of a different status, or should they be held separately in relatively crowded and ill-resourced conditions? Should women be held locally, in prisons catering largely for men, so that they can easily receive visits? Or should they be accommodated in more distant specialized establishments catering exclusively for women and providing a superior range of facilities but which it is more difficult for their visitors to reach? These are fundamental dilemmas, but arguably they should be resolved as much by prisoners and their families as by Prison Service managers. If prisoners are provided with full information about the facilities that different institutions provide, there is no reason why they should not exercise responsible choice, providing the choice is not between equally unacceptable options (which is why there must be minimum standards of provision). Further, there is no reason why prisoner choices cannot be met by organizing queues for the most popular options.

Or, to take another example, prisoners are currently required to work (Prison Rule 28) and may be disciplined for refusing to do so (Prison Rule 47 (18)). In fact, many prisoners would welcome the opportunity of a proper job: many prisoners held in local prisons are not given the option of work; until very recently, sewing mailbags was one of the most common forms of prisoner employment and a high proportion of prisoners are still employed on make-weight domestic cleaning tasks.[30] Should prisoners be given the option of working, pursuing educational or training courses, or remaining idle? Why should their choice not be guided by financial and other incentives as it is for citizens in the community? Does it make sense to create unappealing and meaningless jobs for prisoners merely because the Prison Rules require that they should be given employment when arguably their prospects on release would be better prepared for were a higher proportion of prisoners given the opportunity to gather life and other skills? This debate has only just begun.

Conclusion

Successive inquiries into the prison system in England and Wales have concluded that many of its problems are in large measure a product of our having allowed prisons to become cultural as well as physical enclaves, cut off from the criminal justice system and the community of which they should be an integral part. The standards of service delivered in prisons – health, education, training, employment and so on – got out of kilter with those prevailing elsewhere. Staff working practices became inflexible and restrictive. Justice stopped at the prison gates. Prisoners were dealt with according to, at worst, an authoritarian, and at best, a paternalistic philosophy of treatment and training long since detached from any defensible rationale. After a period of drift during which the prison system lurched from crisis to crisis, there appears now to be a new consensus about what the purpose of the prison system should be. At its core is the concept of the responsible prisoner, who remains a citizen and who retains those rights that Parliament has not expressly taken away and who should be dealt with justly and with humanity. This means, *inter alia*, that standards of fairness should prevail and that decisions should be made with due process: the criteria should be accessible and the reasons given.

The reasoning is that prisoners may thereby have at least the opportunity and encouragement of making positive use of an institution, the primary purpose of which is frankly not positive for those who undergo it. If held captive with dignity and justice the theory is that prisoners' respect for themselves and for the values of the society that imprisoned them will not be irremediably undermined and thus crime will best be prevented. That is the theory: before the theory is tested we have first to establish the practice.

Notes

1   R. Walmesley, L. Howard and S. White, *The National Prison Survey: main findings* (London, HMSO, 1992); J. Gunn, A. Maden and M. Swinton, *Mentally Disordered Prisoners* (London, Institute of Psychiatry, 1991).

2   Home Office, *Prison Statistics England and Wales* (Cmd 1221, HMSO, London, 1990).

3   R. King and R. Morgan, *The Future of the Prison System* (Farnborough, Gower, 1980).

4   S. Brody, *The Effectiveness of Sentencing*, Home Office Research Study No. 35, (London, HMSO, 1976).

5   American Friends Service Committee, *Struggle for Justice: A Report on Crime and Punishment in America* (New York, Hill and Wang, 1971).

6 G. Zellick, 'The Prison Rules and the Courts', *Criminal Law Review* (1981), p. 602; M. Maguire, J. Vagg and R. Morgan (eds.), *Accountability and Prisons: Opening up a Closed World* (London, Tavistock, 1985).

7 May Committee, *Report of the Committee of Inquiry into the United Kingdom Prison Services* (Cmd 7673, London, HMSO, 1979), paras 4.24 and 4.28.

8 Prison Reform Trust, *Prison Rules: A Working Guide* (London, Prison Reform Trust, 1993).

9 Prime Minister, *Efficiency and Effectiveness in the Civil Service* (London, HMSO, 1982).

10 C. Train, 'Management Accountability in the Prison Service' in M. Maguire, J. Vagg and R. Morgan (eds.) op. cit.

11 I. Dunbar, *A Sense of Direction* (London, Prison Service, 1985). The 1984 Home Office report referred to is: *Managing the Long-Term Prison System: the Report of the Control Review Committee* (London, HMSO).

12 *Prison Disturbances April 1990: Report of an Inquiry by the Rt. Hon. Lord Justice Woolf (Parts I and II) and His Honour Judge Stephen Tumin (Part II)*, (Cmd 1456, London, HMSO, 1991).

13 Ibid., para 10.29.

14 Ibid., para 14.8.

15 Ibid., para 10.19.

16 S. K. Ruck (ed.), *Paterson on Prisons: Being the Collected Papers of Sir Alexander Paterson* (London, Arthur Muray, 1951), p. 23.

17 Home Office, *Managing the Long-Term Prison System: the Report of the Control Review Committee*, para 108.

18 R. Morgan, 'Just prisons and responsible prisoners' in A. Duff and S. Marshall (eds.), *Penal Theory and Penal Practice* (Manchester University Press, 1994).

19 N. Morris, *The Future of Imprisonment* (Chicago, University of Chicago Press, 1974).

20 R. Morgan, 'Imprisonment' in M. Maguire, R. Morgan and R. Reiner (eds.), *The Oxford Handbook of Criminology* (Oxford University Press, 1993.

21 For a graphic example see Her Majesty's Chief Inspector of Prisons, *H.M. Prison Cardiff* (London, Home Office, 1993).

22 Woolf Report, op. cit., para 10.69.

23 Ibid., paras 12.1223 and 12.1229.

24 See Home Office, *Prison Statistics England and Wales, 1989* (Cmd 1221, London, HMSO, 1990), chapter 9.

25 E. Genders and E. Player, *Grendon: the Study of a Therapeutic*

Community within the Prison System, A Report to the Home Office (Oxford, Oxford Centre for Criminological Research, 1989).

26 Prison Reform Trust, *Sex Offenders in Prison* (London, Prison Reform Trust, 1990).

27 Home Office, *Custody, Care and Justice : the Way Ahead for the Prison Service in England and Wales* (Cmd 1647, London, HMSO, 1991), paras. 7.35–7.

28 E. Goffman, *Asylums* (Harmondsworth, Penguin, 1968).

29 Home Office, *Custody, Care and Justice*, p. 47.

30 Home Office, *Report of the Work of the Prison Service April 1990–March 1991* (Cmd 1724, London, HMSO, 1991), paras. 55–84.

7

Open Adoption – the Way Forward?

JOHN WILLIAMS

Adoption is a creature of legislation, as under the common law the legal responsibilities of parenthood are inalienable. Salter J said in *Brooks* v. *Blount*,[1]

> I do not think that the person who has custody of a child can be heard to say that he has not such custody unless he has been deprived of it by the order of a competent court.

Prior to the First World War informal arrangements for the substitute care of children by persons other than birth parents were common, especially in Scotland. Although adoption agencies were established to oversee these informal care-arrangements, they lacked any legal basis until the Adoption Act 1926.[2] Following the First World War an increased number of fatherless children were cared for under informal arrange-ments. In its account of the history of adoption, the Hurst Committee identified the difficulties for all concerned in these arrangements.[3] The child lacked the security of knowing that he or she was a full member of the adopting family; the adopters feared the birth mother reclaiming care of the child and the birth mother feared having to resume responsibility for the child if the adopters changed their minds. The lack of permanence was seen to be a crucial weakness in the informal system. It was not until the 1926 Act that a formal legal process which facilitated the transfer of what were then parental rights became available. The changes in the law followed the report by Sir Alfred Hopkinson which recommended the introduction of legal adoption, and the later reports by Tomlin J, whose draft bill formed the basis of the Act.[4]

A more cynical view of the reasons for the introduction of legal adoption was that it was an effective way of transferring financial responsibility for children from the State to private families.[5]

The current law of adoption is found in the Adoption Act 1976 as amended. It is reviewed in the recent White Paper *Adoption: The Future*.[6] The paper emphasizes the need to avoid disruption in the lives of children: adopted children suffer a major disruption which makes it essential that 'Adoption law and adoption policy should ensure as far as possible that an adopted child is not exposed to further disruption . . .'[7] The White Paper concludes that an adoption order when made should be permanent and should not be subject to amendment or dissolution. For the purposes of the law an adoption order serves to terminate the parental responsibility of the birth parent(s) and establish the parental responsibility of the adoptive parents.[8] It also extinguishes any order that may have been in force under the Children Act 1989 as well as any agreement or order to make payments in respect of the child's upbringing or maintenance.[9]

This is the traditional legal framework within which adoption practice has developed. However, some question whether this legal framework and adoption practice should be changed to allow for greater openness in adoption and to encourage, for example, contact between birth parent(s) and a child following adoption. Other forms of openness are mooted in addition to, or as well as, contact. As will be seen below, the law of this country does permit a degree of openness, although some practitioners and most of the judiciary appear cautious in their use of these provisions. This essay explores the idea of open adoption and considers whether or not it should now play a greater part in adoption law and practice. It draws upon the experience of other jurisdictions which have incorporated varying degrees of openness.

Levels of open adoption

The notion that open adoption is a single concept is misleading, as the expression is used to identify different levels of openness. These differences relate to the quality of the openness, and also to the identity of the participants in the openness arrangements. Much of the American literature on open adoption uses the term in an inconsistent manner. For example, Amadio and Deutsch define open adoption in wide terms.

> An open adoption occurs when, prior to the adoption, it is agreed in writing that the child will have continuing contact with one or more members of his or her biological family after the adoption is completed.[10]

A more restrictive definition is provided by Reuben Pannor,

> ... a process in which the birth parents and the adoptive parents meet and exchange identifying information. The birth parents relinquish legal and basic child rearing rights to the adoptive parents. Both sets of parents retain the right of continuing contact and access to knowledge on behalf of the child.[11]

Each of the different levels encompassed within the term raises issues unique to its own classification. However, they all question the traditional assumption of adoption law and practice, namely that adoption is the permanent termination of one relationship with the child and its complete replacement with another. Watson takes an alternative view. His conviction about the value of openness 'stems from accepting the premise ... that children who are adopted always belong to two families. One family gives them their genes, their ancestors and their life; the other their nurture, their protection, and the basic environment in which they develop.'[12] This is echoed by Ryburn, who refers to the legal fiction that adoption extinguishes all ties between a child and its birth family 'so that the illusion was created that the child was a child of its adoptive family *as if by birth*'.[13] These views suggest that policy-makers and practitioners should consider introducing more openness into the adoption process.

A number of possible variants exist within the umbrella term 'open adoption'. For ease of reference they may be illustrated by Table 1. This table cannot be regarded as an exhaustive statement of the variations in openness. It does, however, illustrate the generality of the concept and would allow most,

Table 1: 'Open adoption' variations

Level of openness	Nature of openness	Possibilities within level
Level 1	Information – adult to adult	• Identifying • Non identifying • Pre-adoption • At the time of adoption • Post-adoption
Level 2	Information – adult to child	• Adoptive status • Identifying • Non-identifying • Ongoing
Level 3	Contact – between adult parties	• Adoptive parent(s) – biological parent(s) without child's knowledge • Adoptive parents – biological parent(s) with child knowledge • Pre-adoption • Post-adoption
Level 4	Contact – between child and biological family	• Child–parent(s) • Child–adult relatives (e.g. grandparents) • Child–siblings

if not all, people to agree with some elements of open adoption. Clearly, a number of sensitive issues arise from the above. One crucial matter is the desirability of information exchange and/or contact between adult parties without the knowledge, consent or involvement of the child. In some respects these arrangements run counter to the welfare principle in the Children Act 1989 which emphasizes the importance of involving children in decisions which affect their lives.[14] However, it can be argued that such arrangements may be appropriate as a preliminary to involving the child at some future occasion.

The extent to which information is exchanged, or contact arranged, between potential adoptive parents and natural parents prior to adoption may threaten the more traditional approach to the adoption process. Ryburn is critical of the lack of information passing prior to adoption[15]. He is even more censorious of the extent to which social workers and other professionals control any information which does pass between the parties to the adoption. Basing his argument on the New Zealand *pakeha* (white) adoption he concludes,

> The programme of self-assessment [by adoptive parents], set alongside a system of birth parent choice [of adoptive parents] and openness in placements represents an attempt to empower the parties to adoption themselves. It marks a radical departure from a model in which the social worker is expert, and re-shapes the social work task as one of negotiation and facilitation.[16]

Ryburn is quite clear that such a radical change requires the challenging of a number of myths surrounding the adoption process, most importantly the notion of an objective assessment of the suitability of an adoption placement. Others disagree with this approach. Byrd states that

> Confidential adoptions provide opportunities for adoptive parents to nurture children as their own and in turn allow those children to internalise a single set of parental values. Open adoption allows the involvement of birth parents who may offer a differing set of values.[17]

Perhaps the extremes of this debate can be reconciled, or at least more appropriately discussed, if account is taken of the variety of factual scenarios which may arise. A number of factors may influence whether open or confidential pre-adoption procedures are appropriate – these include the age of the child, the background to the adoption (child abuse, ill health etc.), the wishes of the child and the wishes of the potential adopters and the birth parent(s).

Pre-adoption information sharing and contact may take a variety of forms. One interesting development is that of the adoptive parents being present at the birth of the child. In a study of 1,396 adoptive families in California it was discovered that 15 per cent of adoptive parents were present in the delivery room and a further 15 per cent were nearby in the hospital.[18] These total figures hide a wide diversity of practice between independent adoptions[19] (29% in delivery room, 24% nearby) and agency placements (3% and 6%). Indeed the study revealed

Table 2: California study of adoptive families, 1991

Practice	Total %	Independent %	Agency %
1. Adoptive parents were offered			
Meeting with birth parent	57	75	41
Ongoing contact	48	61	36
2. Adoptive parents met birth parent			
No	31	13	48
Yes	69	87	38
3. Planned for openness at time of placement			
No	47	31	62
Yes	53	69	38
4. Have had post-placement contact			
No	42	22	60
Yes	58	78	40
By mail	45	61	30
By phone	41	60	23
In person	35	41	30

a greater openness in independent placements than in agency ones.

Direct comparisons between the California system and that which applies in England or Wales must be made with caution. However, the findings provide some support for Ryburn's view that professionals tend to steer the parties towards more confidential adoption whereas 'negotiated' adoptions are more likely to lead to openness.

Open adoption under existing law in England and Wales

(i) Access to information

Under the Adoption Agencies Regulations 1983[20] details of the child's personal history and background (including religious and cultural background) will be provided for prospective adopters. If the adoption goes ahead, a written report of the child's health history and current state of health will be sent to the adopters' doctor. Although the regulations are vague this information will probably contain some reference to the health status of the birth parent(s). Difficulties arise in practice when information relating to the child's health status only comes to light at some time after the adoption. At present there is no formal mechanism for conveying such information to the adoptive parents and the adopted child, although the *Review* recommends that a system should be introduced.[21] Identifying information (photographs, school and other reports, letters, etc.) may be exchanged exclusively between birth parent(s) and the adoptive parents, or it may be shared with the child. It is possible that exchanges of information may be kept from the child until he or she is of sufficient understanding.

Perhaps the most radical provision in practice is the procedure for the disclosure of birth records to the adopted child upon reaching the age of eighteen years. The Registrar General is charged with the duty of keeping records of all adoptions in England and Wales.[22] An adopted person who has attained the age of eighteen may apply to the Registrar General for such information contained on the register which will enable him or her to obtain a copy of their birth certificate. This provision was introduced as a result of the recommendation made by the Houghton Committee in 1972.[23] Prior to the Children Act 1975 this information was only available in England and Wales through an order of the High Court or the court which made the adoption order, although in Scotland it was available as of right to any adopted person who had reached the age of seventeen years. In the working paper[24] leading up to the report the Houghton Committee was minded to retain the status quo in England and Wales and to review the position in Scotland in the light of research that was underway. However, the Scottish research indicated that access to this information was of some value to adopted people.[25] As the Houghton Committee favoured greater openness it recommended in the final Report that 'an adopted person aged 18 years or over should be entitled to a copy of his original birth certificate'.

The recommendation was implemented in the Children Act 1975 and the relevant statutory provision is now found in s. 51 of the 1976 Act.[26] Under this section an application must be made to the Registrar General who will then supply the information necessary to enable the person to obtain a copy of the birth certificate. However, the implications of obtaining this information and the ability to use it to trace the birth parent(s) were recognized by the inclusion of a duty to inform the applicant that counselling services are available. In the case of a person adopted prior to 12 November 1975[27] the Registrar General cannot disclose the information unless that person has in fact made use of the counselling services. Until 1989 it was generally assumed that Parliament had intended that the right to this information was absolute. It was not until the Court of Appeal decision in R v. Registrar General, ex parte Smith[28] that its absolute quality was questioned. Smith was a double killer who had been adopted at the age of nine weeks. One of his victims was his cell mate in Broadmoor Hospital whom he believed to be his adoptive mother. He applied to the Registrar General under s. 51 of the 1976 Act; the Registrar decided, after considering medical evidence, not to release the details. There was a fear that Smith's natural mother would be at risk if he managed to trace her. In an action for judicial review both the Divisional Court and the Court of Appeal upheld the Registrar's decision. Their reasoning was that Parliament could not have intended that adopted persons should have an absolute right to access regardless of the circumstances. However, as Le Sueur points out,[29] during the Parliamentary debate on what is now s. 51, reference was made to the very quandary which the *Smith* case identified. Parliament adopted the approach that such issues should be resolved through the statutory counselling process rather than by qualifying the legal right to the information. Regardless of the correctness of the *Smith* decision it remains a binding Court of Appeal authority which provides the Registrar General with an undefined discretion. A number of potential problems exist. Would it be sufficient reason to refuse to provide details if it was suspected that the adopted person might then blackmail the birth parent(s)? What standard of proof is required before the Registrar is persuaded that it is in the public interest not to disclose the details?[30] No ready answers are available. The *Smith* case illustrates a particular problem with open adoption, namely, that of reconciling the rights, wishes or needs of the parties in the adoption triad. Potential conflict is not confined to the time of adoption.

Changes to the 1976 Act introduced by the Children Act 1989 provided additional assistance for adopted people wishing to trace their natural relatives. The Registrar General is required to keep an Adoption Contact Register which is designed to facilitate the tracing of relatives. An adopted person who has reached the age of eighteen years may, subject to certain conditions, enter his or her name on the Adoption Contact Register. Relatives[31] of an adopted person may also register their names and addresses on the Register. The Registrar General must inform the registered adopted person of the name and address of any relative whose name is also included on the register; where requested, the address may be a third-party address. Relatives may also make use of an intermediary such as an experienced adoption counsellor.[32] It is up to the respective individuals to determine the extent and quality of any contact.

The above developments in the law are well intended and in many cases will provide much comfort to adopted children and their birth families. In that respect they are welcome. However, they also reveal an inherent contradiction in adoption practice. If it is considered desirable that an adopted child is eventually able to discover the identity of his or her birth parents, are there any benefits in delaying the exercise of this right until the eighteenth birthday? The passage of time between adoption and attaining the age of majority *may* allow hostility to develop, fantasies to emerge and fears to multiply. Suddenly trying to establish a relationship between two people who may be strangers *may* be difficult and traumatic. It must be emphasized that these *may* be the consequences of this policy – they are not inevitable. Nevertheless, the potential for damaging meetings and relationships is there and must invite consideration of alternative methods of achieving the laudable objectives of the above statutory provision. Greater openness during minority is clearly one way in which they may be achieved.

(ii) Access and contact conditions in adoption orders
Section 12(5) Adoption Act 1976 states that an adoption order may contain such terms and conditions as the court thinks fit. Although this may appear to give the courts wide discretion in attaching terms and conditions, the judiciary has exercised considerable caution in making use of the power. The judges place great emphasis on the permanent transfer of parental responsibility. Terms and conditions attached to an adoption order prima facie threaten both the permanency and the transfer. In *Re M (a minor) (adoption order: access)*[33] the Court of Appeal held that to compel adoptive parents to grant members of the birth family access to the child would interfere with their rights and duties in respect of the child. Enforcing such a condition would give rise to problems which could undermine the new relationship. The Court went further and said that even if the adoptive parents were to allow

access great caution must be exercised as circumstances might change. Oliver LJ in *Re V (a minor) (adoption: consent)*[34] had difficulty in reconciling the need to secure stability for the child whilst also seeking to give a birth parent regular and frequent access. He said,

> Once it is found, however, that regular and frequent access, inevitably maintaining and strengthening the family ties between the child and his mother and her other children, is so conducive to the welfare of the child that provision has to be made for it in the adoption order as the underlying basis on which the order is made at all, I find it difficult to reconcile that with the avowed purpose of the adoption of extinguishing any parental rights or duties in the natural parents.

A slightly different tone is adopted when considering access between the adopted child and a relative other than a parent. In *Re C (a minor) (adoption: conditions)*[35] the House of Lords drew a distinction (albeit one of degree) between access by birth parents and access by other blood relatives. These other relatives have no parental rights and duties to be transferred upon adoption; therefore, argued their Lordships, the same complicating factors do not arise. These three cases represent the traditional approach of the judges towards the effects of adoption. Under s. 37 Children Act 1975 a court could direct that an adoption application was to be treated as an application for custodianship. Custodianship was an intermediate status between care and control of a child and full adoption. Unlike adoption, custodianship did not transfer full parental rights and duties, nor was it necessarily permanent. It was designed to provide a legal framework for long-term carers of a child in cases where adoption was inappropriate (for example, grandparents seeking to adopt).[36] In practice there was very little enthusiasm for custodianship and it was rarely used.

The Children Act 1989 made a number of important changes to the law. Firstly, it abolished custodianship. Secondly, when making an adoption order the court may include a contact order under the 1989 Act. A contact order widens the old concept of access; it includes not only visits but also letters, telephone calls, birthday presents and other forms of contact. The abolition of custodianship has very little effect. In its place the court has the power to make a residence order as an alternative to adoption.[37] However, the express power to include a contact order in an adoption order provides adoption practitioners and the judiciary with the opportunity to rethink attitudes on greater openness in adoption. The judicial caution shown in *Re M*, *Re V* and *Re C* no longer appears appropriate. In spite of this clear signal to the judiciary there appears to be no enthusiasm for greater openness through the use of contact orders. Open adoption has been raised as an issue in a number of recent cases.[38] In *Re D (a minor)*[39] the Court of Appeal pointed out, quite rightly, that a prerequisite to open adoption was the consent and co-operation of the adopting parents. This was also recognized by Butler-Sloss LJ in *Re R (a minor)*[40] where she said that a contact order can 'in theory at least' now be *imposed* on adopters as an alternative to making an order with conditions. Thorpe J in *Re C (a minor) (adopted child: contact)*[41] held that a substantive application for a contact order in an adoption case would fall to be determined according to the principles laid down by the House of Lords in *Re C [1988]*. This latter case, if followed, reinforces the traditional view of adoption and fails to seize the opportunity provided by the Children Act 1989.

(iii) Adoption: the future – the White Paper proposals
The White Paper is the first major review of adoption law and practice since the 1970s and it recognizes the changing background to adoption. One significant feature is the decline in the number of children adopted. In 1977 (the year after the Adoption Act 1976) 13,000 children were adopted, whereas in 1991 that figure was just over 7,000.[42] The number of young babies placed for adoption has declined as a consequence of better contraception and the changes in attitude to lone parent families. However, the number of older children available for adoption has declined less than that of younger children. As the

White Paper points out, matching older children with adoptive parents is more difficult and post-adoption contact may be more appropriate. Nevertheless, the White Paper stresses that the most important objective once an adoption order is made is to support the new family relationship.[43]

In those cases where birth parents wish to maintain direct contact then, provided the adoptive family and the child agree, the White Paper recommends that it should generally be allowed. Where adoptive parents object, their views should have greater weight than those of the birth parent(s), although this will need careful judgement in the case of an older child who has formed a bond with the birth parent(s). In the spirit of the Children Act 1989 the White Paper emphasizes that each case should be decided on its own facts and that new regulations will ensure that courts and adoption agencies will always assess the most suitable arrangements for post-adoption contact.[44]

Open adoption in other jurisdictions

(i) New Zealand[45]

As noted above, New Zealand has developed a high level of openness in adoption. Its early adoption laws recognized the right to identifying information. Traditional Maori adoption did not regard adoption as a method by which unwanted children were cared for by substitute parents. Provision of companionship, comforting a childless couple and the passing of knowledge from one generation to another provided the motive for many Maori adoptions. Adopted children continued to have access to their natural parents. This traditional form of adoption influenced the *pakeha* adoption, which is based on an assumption of continuing contact between birth parent(s) and the child. Birth parents have a significant say in the choice of adoptive parents; potential adopters and birth parent(s) discuss and agree the nature of post-adoption contact; adopters and parents are empowered and professionals play a facilitating role rather than make objective assessments.

(ii) France[46]

French law allows two forms of adoption – full adoption and limited adoption. Full adoption represents a complete transfer of parental rights to the adopters. The child takes the adopters' name and is a member of the adoptive family in respect of whom the rights of succession apply. This form of adoption has much in common with our own adoption law and practice. Limited adoption was in part a response to the growing number of older children being placed for adoption. It differs radically from full adoption as the child retains his or her links with the birth family, although the natural parents' duty to maintain is secondary to that of the adoptive parents, and parental authority is transferred to the adopters. The child will retain his or her name, but the adoptive family name may be added. In effect the child has a 'double relationship'.[47] Limited adoption is revocable. In some respects limited adoption is similar to a residence order under the Children Act 1989. However, one important difference is that under a residence order the birth parent(s) will not lose parental responsibility by virtue of the order being made.[48]

(iii) United States of America

A number of states in America allow varying degrees of openness in adoption. Reforms in the law have been 'piecemeal and fragmentary'.[49] Within America the debate on openness has been influenced by the problem of 'foster care drift', in which children remain in foster care for considerable periods of time with little, if any, thought being given to permanent future arrangements.[50] In response to this problem the 'Permanency Program' was developed which sought to get children out of foster care as soon as possible. This could be achieved either by returning the child to his or her parents or by terminating parental rights and placing the child for adoption. Rather than concentrate on improving the quality of foster care, the programme concentrated more on achieving a settled and permanent future. The programme relies heavily on the writing of Goldstein, Freud and Solnit.[51] They argued that permanency in the child/parent relationship was a paramount requirement of development. What was important for a child was the *psychological* parent rather than the birth one. They state,

> Children have difficulty in relating positively to, profiting from, and maintaining contact with two psychological parents who are not in positive contact with each other. Loyalty conflicts are common and normal under such conditions and may have devastating consequences by destroying a child's positive relationship to both parents. A 'visiting' or 'visited' parent has little chance to serve as a true object for love, trust, and identification, since the role is based on his being available on an uninterrupted day to day basis.[52]

Garrison points out the inconsistency between the enthusiasm for the Goldstein et al. approach in relation to long-term foster care and the reluctance to embrace their identical argument in relation to custody following divorce.[53] When addressing the issue of adoption Garrison refers to studies which indicate that adopted children may suffer the same problems of confused identity, insecurity and guilt that children in long-term foster care encounter.[54] She concludes that

> Adoption by itself cannot resolve the emotional problems that these experiences [family breakdown or inadequate parental care] produce. Thus, as older children with more substantial ties to their natural parents have moved into the 'adoption marketplace', failed adoptions – children who are returned by their prospective adoptive parents – have increased.
>
>   The child's natural parent and his previous family experiences remain important even if he lives in a loving permanent home. The child must somehow come to terms with his past, and the available evidence suggests that he is better able to do so if his natural parent remains a live presence rather than a fantasy.[55]

Garrison's tentative assertions are confirmed by the California study of 1,396 adoptive families referred to above. This is one of the very few large-scale surveys of openness in adoption and its results, even in relation to agency adoptions, are on the whole favourably disposed to the idea. In her account of the project Berry puts forward the following conclusions:[56]

- Adoptive parents perceive themselves to be in some control of the situation – but the lack of complete control does not prevent them from practising openness or feeling satisfied with the adoption.
- The majority of adoptions involved an offer of openness.
- Agency adopters are more likely to have a negative impression of the birth parents.
- Children in open adoptions are rated higher than closed adoption children in regard to all behaviour dimensions when rating child behaviour.

The findings indicate, she concludes, 'that openness is a somewhat cautious, but satisfactory, situation for many adoptive parents'.[57] This realistic assessment of the effectiveness of open adoption is welcome. It removes the debate beyond the entrenched positions of those who advocate it as a panacea and those who regard it as a complete anathema.

Cook[58] examines the American case and statute law, and the implications for the State in open adoption. His survey finds that the law continues to emphasize confidentiality and the complete severance of the rights, responsibilities and privileges of the natural family. Although premised on the 'best interests of the child', this approach, he argues, may in some cases be positively harmful to those interests. He states that

> ... it cannot be said that the child's best interests are safeguarded in cases in which the adoptee and the natural family already enjoy an established relationship at the time of adoption. In such cases, has not the letter of the law achieved an awkward supremacy over the spirit of the law?[59]

The arguments for and against openness in adoption

Proponents and opponents of greater openness in adoption have identified the arguments for and against with a remarkable degree of clarity, but little common ground has been established. A tendency towards total commitment to one side of the argument or the other has often led to the best interests or welfare of individual children in the adoption process being subsumed by the need to retain the purity of an argument. These respective arguments may be conveniently summarized by reference to the individual parties to the adoption triangle.

(i) The birth parent(s)

Much of the argument surrounding the birth parent concentrates on the grief which may be experienced both during and following the adoption. Two schools of thought exist. There are those who argue that the grieving process is assisted by greater openness because the birth parent(s) know that they will not lose contact with the child, or that they will receive information as to how the child is progressing. This may ease feelings of guilt and encourage a more positive attitude to the child and the adoptive parents. The contrary argument is that ongoing contact or information may serve as a constant reminder of the child or as a 'stimulus for the fantasy that relinquishing a child is not really a loss at all'.[60]

An open adoption may benefit the birth parent(s) by giving them some degree of control over the adoption of their child and allowing them to visualize the new family environment. Again this can lead to less guilt and uncertainty. On the other hand, the potential benefits of open adoption may pressurize the parent(s) to place a child for adoption where they would not otherwise have done so. Instead of easing guilt, open adoption may in fact create 'ambivalence and confusion' for the birth mother.[61]

(ii) Adoptive parents

As far as adoptive parents are concerned, the discussion concentrates on the effects of openness on the bonding or attachment process. It is argued that openness may inhibit this process and work to the detriment of the adoptive parents. They are constantly reminded that the child is 'not theirs'; they may be unsure and constantly trying to second guess what the birth parent(s) would think of their exercise of parental responsibility. One further problem identified by Sibler and Dorner[62] is that of the birth parent(s) becoming dependent on the adoptive family and seeing themselves as part of an extended family unit.

Adoptive parents may benefit from openness as it removes the secrecy behind the adoption and avoids a situation whereby the professionals and the courts are the people who hold all the information. This may increase their control of the process. One further point is that open adoption may increase the number of children placed for adoption and thus fulfil the desire of many potential adopters.[63]

(iii) The child

If open adoption is to be seen as a way forward then it must be shown positively to benefit the child. Clearly, the effects on the adults – especially, but not exclusively – the adoptive parents will have implications for the child. Byrd opines that, 'in open adoption, adolescent adoptees are likely to vacillate between different sets of parents – moving helplessly through a cycle of unresolved conflicts.'[64] It is argued that closed adoption provides the child with an 'incomplete identity' and prevents the child from acquiring a single set of values.[65] A true understanding of the nature of adoption at too early a stage in life may mean that the child is unable to cope and feels insecure in the new family.[66]

Advocates of greater openness point to the confusion caused for the child by confidential or closed adoption. The child does not have to delay 'searching out' the birth parent(s) until attaining the age of majority, with all the potential traumas which that may involve. In cases of children whose parents are divorced, the Children Act 1989 recognizes that continued contact and involvement by the non-resident parent are an important part of the child's development. Although adoption is different from post-divorce settlements, there is no compelling reason why the principle of continued contact and involvement should be automatically excluded following adoption.

Conclusion

It is submitted that the case for greater openness in adoption is well founded, although not of universal application. Between total confidentiality and complete openness there is a wide range of possibilities, any one of which may prove to be in the best interests of a child. The debate must move from one of extreme standpoints to one which recognizes the appropriateness of a flexible approach to openness in adoption and one which is prepared to respond to the individual needs of a child. As the California study illustrates, open adoption has proved to be a positive experience for many adoptive families. At the same time it recognizes that for some adoptive families it has been a negative experience. What is required is an approach that obliges professionals and courts, but more importantly empowers and enables birth parent(s) and potential adopters, to explore the possibilities of incorporating a level of openness in the adoption. Adoption agencies may find that their role is changing from that of a manager to that of a facilitator encouraging negotiated adoptions where appropriate. Flexibility is the key to such an approach. The White Paper makes some movement towards greater flexibility, although it lacks a complete commitment to greater openness.

No two adoptions are identical. The personalities, hopes and desires of the parties to the adoption triad will vary. It is essential that all parties concentrate on the welfare of the child concerned, and take account of his or her age, background, views, expectations and needs. These are the factors which should influence the nature of the specific adoption. To some adults this may appear to be a retrograde step and represent the demise of adoption as we know it; to others it may be a welcome reform. However, for children it will increase the chances that they will receive the most appropriate type of placement, and reduce the risk of the adults getting it wrong.

Notes

1 (1923) 87 JP 64.

2 In Scotland adoption was not formalized until the Adoption (Scotland) Act 1930.

3 *Report of the Departmental Committee on the Adoption of Children* (Cmd 9248, HMSO, 1984) para. 12.

4 Sir Alfred Hopkinson, *Report of the Committee on Child Adoption* (Cmd 1254, HMSO, 1921); *Child Adoption Committee First Report* (Cmd 2401, HMSO, 1925) and *Child Adoption Committee Second Report* (Cmd 2469, HMSO, 1925).

5 See H. Kirk and S. McDaniels, 'Adoption policy and practice in Great Britain and North America', Vol. 13, *Journal of Social Policy*, pp. 75–84.

6 *Adoption: The Future* (HMSO, Cmd 2288).

7 Ibid., para. 4.5.

8 S. 12 Adoption Act 1976.

9 S. 12(3).

10 C. Amadio and S. Deutsch, 'Open adoption: allowing adopted children to "stay in touch" with blood relatives', *Journal of Family Law*, Vol. 22 (1984), pp. 58–93.

11 See D. Byrd, 'The case for confidential adoption', *Public Welfare* (1988), pp. 20–3 at p. 20.

12 K. Watson, 'The case for open adoption', *Public Welfare* (1988), pp. 24–8.

13 M. Ryburn, 'Openness in adoption', Vol. 14, *Adoption and Fostering* (1990), pp. 21–6 at p. 21.

14 See s. 1 Children Act 1989.

15 Op. cit. p. 22. See also D. Howell and R. Murray, 'New Zealand: new ways to choose adopters', Vol. 11, *Adoption and Fostering* (1987), pp. 38–41.

16 Ibid., p. 26.

17 Op. cit., p. 22.

18 M. Berry, 'The practice of open adoption: findings from a study of 1,396 adoptive families', Vol. 13, *Children and Youth Service Review* (1991), pp. 379–95.

19 Defined as an adoption initiated without an agency, although some public review of the arrangements takes place.

20 r 11, 12 & 14 S.I. 1984 No. 1964.

21 *Review of Adoption Law – Report to Ministers of an Inter-departmental Working Group* (Department of Health and Welsh Office, October 1992). See also para. 4.26 White Paper.

22 S. 51 Adoption Act 1976.

23 Sir Williams Houghton, *Report of the Departmental Committee on the Adoption of Children* (HMSO 1972, Cmnd 5107). See paras. 300–6 and Recommendation 78.

24 *Adoption of Children, Departmental Committee on the Adoption of Children* (HMSO, 1970).

25 J. Triseliotis, *In Search of Origins* (Routledge and Keegan Paul, 1973).

26 S. 51(2) enables an adopted person under the age of eighteen years who is intending to marry to check with the Registrar General whether the intended spouse falls within the prohibited degrees of relationship under the 1949 Marriage Act. No further information may be disclosed under this subsection.

27 The date on which the 1975 Children Act was passed by Parliament.

28 [1990] 2 All ER 170 (Divisional Court); [1991] 2 All ER 782 (Court of Appeal).

29 A. P. Le Sueur, *Unruly Horses and the Adoption Act*, (1991) 3 JCL pp. 129–31.

30 Ibid., p. 131.

31 The term 'relative' is defined as 'any person (other than an adoptive relative) who is related to the adopted person by blood (including half-blood) or marriage' – S. 51A Adoption Act, 1976.

32 See para. 5 Circular No. LAC (91)9 – *The Children Act 1989: Adoption Contact Register*. One such counselling organization is the National Organization for the Counselling of Adoptees.

33 [1986] 1 FLR 51.

34 [1986] 1 All ER 752.

35 [1988] 1 All ER 705 HL.

36 See Houghton, para. 116 and J. Williams, 'Custodianship and Adoption', *Journal of Social Welfare Law* (1988), pp. 250–62.

37 See S. 8 Children Act 1989.

38 See for example *Re R (a minor)* Court of Appeal 15 June 1993 and *Salford and Manchester CC v. Englehard and Others* Court of Appeal 29 April 1993.

39 [1992] 1 FCR 461.

40 Court of Appeal 15 June 1993 (transcript John Larking).

41 [1993] 3 All ER 259.

42 Op. cit., para. 3.2–3.3.

43 Ibid., para. 4.14.

44 Ibid., para. 4.16.

45 See notes 11 and 13.

46 See P. Verdier, 'Limited adoption in France', Vol. 12, *Adoption and Fostering* (1988), pp. 41–4.

47 Ibid., p. 42.

48 S. 2(6) Children Act 1989.
49 P. Sachdev, 'Achieving openness adoption – some critical issues in policy formulation', Vol. 61, *American Journal of Orthopsychiatry* (1991), pp. 241–9.
50 For a detailed account of this debate in relation to long-term foster care see M. Garrison, 'Why terminate parental rights?', Vol. 35, *Stanford Law Review* (1983), pp. 423–96.
51 J. Goldstein, A. Freud and A. Solnit, *Beyond the Best Interests of the Child* (Goldstein, New York, 1981) and *Before the Best Interests of the Child* (Goldstein, New York, 1979).
52 *Beyond the Best Interests*, p. 39.
53 Op. cit., p. 453. See also Dembitz, 'Beyond Any Discipline's Competence', Vol. 83, *Yale Law Journal* (1974), p. 1304.
54 Ibid., p. 470 and n. 217.
55 Ibid., pp. 472–3.
56 Op. cit., pp. 392–3.
57 Ibid.
58 L. W. Cook, 'Open adoption: can visitation with natural family members be in the child's best interests?', Vol. 30, *Journal of Family Law* (1991–2), pp. 471–93.
59 Ibid., pp. 591–2.
60 See Byrd, op. cit., p. 20.
61 See Berry, op. cit., p. 641.
62 K. Silber and P. M. Dorner, *Children of Open Adoption* (Corona Publishing Co., 1989).
63 See generally Berry, op. cit., p. 638.
64 Op. cit., p. 23.
65 See n. 11 above.
66 See Berry, op. cit., p. 641.

8

Practice and Research: Some Reflections

JILL PEAY

It is a familiar refrain amongst criminologists that there is a difference between 'the law in books' and 'the law in action'. Equally familiar is the assertion that the personnel of the criminal justice process – lawyers, justices, judges and the police to name but a few – are ill-equipped for their roles. Sometimes, criminologists frustratedly allege that these key participants are not even fully aware of the statutory provisions and regulations they are required to apply, leading to more than a suspicion that the professionals are not playing the game by the rules and/or that they are not up to the job.[1] But the frustration and suspicion are mutual. Some practitioners believe that research merely demonstrates that which practitioners already know; and if it fails to do that, then it is based on opinion, assertion and a lack of real understanding of the practitioner's world.[2] These cross-currents surface intermittently, most recently emerging in the acrimonious debate stemming from the Report of the Royal Commission on Criminal Justice (1993) at the British Criminology Conference in Cardiff.[3]

Jane Morgan straddled these two worlds – of academe and practice. She encouraged me, as she did others, to expand my horizons and lent her support during my transition from academic to pupil barrister. The gulf between the professions is one about which I, too, am now sensitive. But, it is one which I intend to address only in part, and in that part which most intrigues me; namely, the varying mores and imperatives of researchers and barristers.[4] I shall compare and contrast four issues; namely, (i) the pursuit of truth; (ii) notions of independence; (iii) the relevance of rules and adhering to them; and (iv) questions of responsibility. In essence, an erstwhile criminologist peeks across the barricades.

The pursuit of truth

I shall use as my starting point, and as a recurrent theme, David Pannick's authoritative study of the principles, practices and morality of barristers: *Advocates*. Amongst the essentials of the role of barrister, Pannick notes the need to be persuasive on behalf of the person who 'pays' for his or her voice; he cites Frankfurter's crystallization of the advocate's fundamental role as

> ... not to enlarge the intellectual horizon. His task is to seduce, to seize the mind for a predetermined end, not to explore paths to truth.[5]

In contrast, criminology is concerned, as Sutherland and Cressey assert, with that

> ... body of knowledge regarding juvenile delinquency and crime as social phenomena. It includes within its scope the processes of making laws, of breaking laws, and of reacting toward the breaking of laws.[6]

Hence, the subject matter of criminology is this sequence of interactions, or, as Jock Young succinctly put it, 'with crime and the reaction to it' (British Criminology Conference, Cardiff, 1993).

Criminology is, therefore, a broad church. The opportunity to do unhindered and unlimited research is the criminologist's nirvana. Such opportunities are now almost non-existent and were rare in 1980 when Jane and I first met via the Oxford Centre for Criminological Research. Yet, at that time, the Centre benefited from the receipt of a rolling grant from the Home Office, theoretically allowing the researchers at the Oxford Centre to undertake unhindered research. Relative freedom of exploration and the definition of issues worthy of examination were central to our role there. The ability to pose yet one more question or explore another subtlety was open to us; ultimate freedom of expression was to be another issue, but one in the early days by which we felt untouched. Criminology accordingly should concern the full pursuit of an enquiry through to an understanding of some elusive quintessential truth. Research and theory in tandem. In this process the goal traditionally remains out of reach, but is, none the less, striven for.

In contrast, for barristers working within an adversarial system, 'getting at the truth' is not the key imperative. Indeed, exploring the shades of meaning and the borderlines of grey uncertainty – manna to a researcher – are not necessarily on the barrister's check-list and may arise only spasmodically, for example, in the construction of doubt for the consumption of a jury. The barrister's task in pursuing the interests of a client is clearly instrumental; to prove a case in court certain legal elements must be satisfied – the absence of any one in the list of 'duty, breach, damage, causation, foreseeability' could make an action for personal injury on the grounds of negligence an impossibility. So, conferences with clients are structured affairs – not an open-ended meeting of minds. Indeed, much of the groundwork in eliciting facts in support of the client's interests falls to the solicitor, the barrister's buffer.

The full exploration of issues with the client is not an invariable or natural goal for barristers. Although barristers should anticipate both those issues relevant to the client's case, and be alive to those unhelpful facts likely to be produced by the other side, the imperative, even within the confidential setting of a conference, may sometimes be to stop asking questions at a point at which counsel has an answer with which she can work. This imperative applies most compellingly in respect of public testimony, where baby barristers are repeatedly warned of the dangers of asking one more question – which may prove to be their downfall if the witness provides an unexpected or unwelcome answer. In criminal matters it may, on occasions, be better to make do with an answer, than push a client into a corner where they say something from which there may be no retracting. 'Did you do it?' is not a question which trips regularly from the lips of criminal practitioners in conference, particularly

given the duty of counsel to advise a client about the merits of a
guilty plea once it becomes evident that the client has no defence
– or no honest defence. As a result, less judgemental enquiries
along the lines of 'What did you do?' or 'What happened?', may
be posed or, more likely still, a series of questions about limited
issues: 'The police say the goods were under your bed – what do
you say?' Undermining the client's confidence in the possibility
of a defence is not the role of the advocate, particularly when
the client wishes to plead not guilty and put the prosecution
to proof.

Hence, to advocate the client's cause may mean remaining in
sheltered ignorance of issues which could readily be explored.
In a particularly complex or long-drawn-out case some issues
may be left until the door of the court, or even later, before
they are finally clarified with a client. Ultimately, such difficult
issues are likely to be the subject of cross-examination by counsel
for the prosecution, and so the defence must, at some point,
prepare for them. But not necessarily early and sometimes
not necessarily at all. Similarly, although no honest barrister
would manufacture a defence for a client, they may seize an
opportunity to explain to a client that a legal defence exists given
the client's instructions. The ultimate objective sets the agenda.
One consequence follows; researchers may be better listeners
than talkers; barristers are certainly better talkers than they are
listeners. The role of researcher may often be thrown into that
of counsellor; but the role of counsel, in stark contrast, is the
instrumental one of procuring a result.[7] Where the authorized
actions of an attorney bring about a result by care or effort the
most apt name is not that of counsel, but that employed by the
Scots – 'Procurator Fiscal'.

The client's instructions, therefore, may be as much constructed
as elicited. Joanna Shapland's work on mitigation – 'a reasoned
argument or exercise in persuasion'[8] – regarded the art of
mitigation as involving actively structuring information for
the sentencer and presenting only that judged realistic. It was
a process of ordering and persuasion. Having observed and
conducted mitigation at first hand I would suggest that the

process of construction takes place at one stage earlier than it was possible for Shapland to observe; barristers seek to prepare a mitigation not on the basis of what clients tell them, but on the basis of what they and their solicitors choose to ask (or refrain from asking) clients.

Independence

Another aspect of unhindered – independent – research concerns the freedom to select the area of inquiry and the definition of key issues. Independence is also crucial to the bar. To be prepared to act for any client, to speak without fear or favour and to adhere to the tenets of the cab rank rule – with all that it implies about access to justice – are central to the barrister's role. So central, that this principle, along with that of a shared duty to the court, is used as a partial justification for the dubious immunity counsel enjoy in court. As Pannick notes, the advocate's duty is to ensure that all that can be said on a client's behalf to the court has been said; in turn, this will assist the court properly to determine the legal rights and duties of relevant persons.[9] The State punishes or imposes other detriments by judging conduct according to predetermined rules.[10] To ascertain whether those rules should apply requires rational debate and hence the very best of advocacy to ensure that the court properly decides where legal right lies for those most affected.

Yet the need for certainty in the law for justice to be seen to be done is partially predicated on the presumption that individuals exercise choice in their actions and omissions. Accordingly, they need full information about the consequences that will stem from their decisions. This is, of course, a popular myth (see generally, Corbett and Simon on rational choice perspective and the concept of 'limited rationality').[11] The offender who says, 'I would never have raped had I known that a life sentence would follow', does not mean this; he means, 'I would not have raped had I been certain that I would have been caught, convicted and sentenced to life imprisonment' – and even then the element of hindsight in this expression of past intent and the potential for deterrence should not be underestimated. The ill-informed client exercising an irrational choice makes a mockery of the need for certainty in the law.

Reasoned debate, as Pannick asserts, is fundamental to the survival of civilized society, even if not all are capable of participating and are reliant on the skills, or lack of them, of others. This, in turn, underpins the irony that it is the very process of taking instructions, and the interactive process it implies, which contributes to the role of barrister as one who constructs a legal case, rather than one who elicits it. Clients may not have the capacity to give instructions merely because they know nothing of the law or the procedures. They may feel themselves morally in the right or wrong, but cannot know with legal certainty. It is for the barrister to 'take instructions', but this does not mean the sharing of legal knowledge to enable the client to decide, but the reflection by the barrister to the client of the options. Curiously, clients seem sometimes to wish to be advised in stark terms. The question is posed, 'What would you do in my place?'. And even when presented with clear options clients may not fully grasp that with which they have concurred – as evidenced by the need for counsel occasionally to stand next to a client pleading to a complicated indictment. Carlen (1976) powerfully detailed the alienation of the subject from the Criminal Justice System. Clients must often feel they are the bit players. Or as Pannick notes: 'The effective performance of the function of the advocate is rarely assisted by the client.'[12]

Curiously, even the client who makes decisions which, though not irrational, do not maximize the advantage to be gleaned from conventional choices, can cause chaos. One of the most recent examples is that noted by Hood, namely, that black defendants are seemingly more likely to enter *late* guilty pleas and accordingly receive more serious sentences than their white counterparts.[13] Yet this reluctance can be readily understood from both the perspective of practice and research; researchers might not wish to gamble on a particular outcome – given the preparedness of players with power in the criminal justice process to depart from their texts; equally, practitioners recognize that the case cannot be proved until the participant witnesses turn up at court.[14]

Accordingly, 'independent' advice emerges in the interaction between barrister, client and their respective knowledge, beliefs, attitudes, experiences and tolerance of risk. The dilemmas posed by the life sentence can illustrate the point. One such client had been convicted of multiple rape and received a number of discretionary life sentences. He wished to appeal with a view to substituting fixed-term sentences – of whatever length – with a pre-determined release date of maximum duration. The prospect of early release has never been sufficient to off-set the perceived disadvantages of indeterminacy, as parole researchers have illustrated,[15] and the client understandably wished for a fixed-term sentence. Yet, with change in the law following *Thynne, Wilson and Gunnell* v. *UK (1989) 190 Series A* European Court of Human Rights, life-sentenced prisoners who are not dangerous cannot be detained beyond their tariff period – in theory. Yet as researchers have demonstrated (not least myself in the mental health context)[16] decision-makers find ways and means to detain those perceived as dangerous. And, after all, dangerousness in the context of mental instability is the basis of the discretionary life sentence *R* v. *Hodgson (1967) 52 Cr App R 113* and *R* v. *Wilkinson (1983) 5 Cr App R (S) 105*. But, in the case in question, the medical experts found the offender to suffer from no psychiatric problems. None the less, the courts took the view that he 'must be mad' to have committed the offences of which he was convicted. But how should the client have been advised? From the perspective of a researcher or lawyer? As a woman or barrister? If we cannot, as sociologists/psychologists remind us, divorce ourselves from our social/personal context, and if we should not, as feminists urge, devalue our own experiences, how can the notion of independent advice exist? Add to this the hurdles and burdens associated with the less than fully informed client and there is a recipe only for a solution negotiated in one guise or another.

Although researchers and barristers share a desire to be independent, attaining this is undoubtedly problematic. The fight being put up by the Bar to prevent rights of audience being extended to the Crown Prosecution Service (CPS) is not, I like to think, motivated by a closed-shop mentality, but by a genuine belief amongst some barristers that the notion of independence is based on a preparedness to represent all clients of whatever means in whatever causes. Although the Lord Chancellor's Advisory Committee on Legal Education and Conduct would have been prepared to recommend to the Lord Chancellor that rights of audience should be extended to solicitors in private practice, the Law Society's application for extended rights foundered on the question of employed solicitors; the committee was not prepared to see rights of audience extended to members of the CPS.[17] The need for a rounded practice, which, it is argued, paid employees of the CPS could never experience, is regarded as critical. It would be trite to observe that some practitioners join the CPS from the independent Bar, the current DPP Barbara Mills being a prime example, and that some practitioners ultimately leave for the Bar. Perhaps, more pertinently, criminologists readily acknowledge that notions of independence are not only ephemeral but also fragile. Independent from what or whom? The CPS are dependent on the police for information and the Bar on the CPS for instructions – and ultimately the same information. Once initially constructed by the police, all who subsequently use that information are tainted by it.[18]

Does independence mean the ability to bring an independent mind? Even if it does, the Bar is not free from suggestions of partiality or its more acceptable face, 'specialization'. There are barristers and sets of chambers undertaking primarily defence/ plaintiff work – and those chambers which are not even offered the opportunity to take prosecution briefs. Moreover, not all do legally-aided work and in a field where legal aid is unobtainable, the best advocacy need not be equitably distributed. Other barristers effectively exclude themselves from particular types of work. The defence of men accused of rape is one such example. Some argue that to do the job properly means being prepared vigorously to cross-examine the victim on issues of consent and, where the rules can be manipulated to meet the situation, about her sexual history. Given the disincentives to reporting rape, some barristers are not prepared to add to the victim's lot in this way.[19] Yet this cannot be the answer. Leaving aside innocent until proven guilty, how does the angst-ridden barrister reconcile a decision not to represent an alleged rapist with a decision to represent other moral outcasts – the alleged murderer/drug manufacturer/corrupter of small children – and to push to the limit the 'no stone unturned/no opportunity not exploited' philosophy. This philosophy may, as a result of their efforts and the exploitation of every leeway in the rules of criminal evidence, result in the acquittal of the guilty. The response goes ... barristers are not there to judge their clients; the determination of guilt is for the jury, the barrister's role is merely to present arguments on behalf of the client. The client is paying for your advocacy, not your judgment. Unlike Lewis Carroll, barristers should not sentence first and convict afterwards. But like Lewis Carroll, they are expected to suspend their disbelief.

Rules

But there is more to it than that. How hard should one try? Do counsel covertly fail to take every point for 'less attractive' clients? And, if so, why do they seemingly feel the need to turn down a brief which would require vigorous cross-examination of an alleged rape victim rather than to treat the victim-witness with respect – namely, not to take every conceivable point?

The Code of Conduct encapsulates the dilemma in its fundamental principles: 'A practising barrister ... must assist the Court in the administration of justice and must not deceive or knowingly or recklessly mislead the court.'[20] This applies equally to facts and law. Pannick puts this requirement in the context of case law:[21] 'consistently with the rule that the prosecution must prove its case, he may passively stand by and watch the court being misled by reason of its failure to ascertain facts that are within the barrister's knowledge' *Saif Ali* v. *Sydney Mitchell & Co (A Firm)* [1980] AC 198, 220.

Frequently, poor prosecution – perhaps the failure to ask for vital documents like a defendant's bank statements or passport – is the fundamental reason for the acquittal. Few practitioners could resist the suggestion that cases are as often lost as they are won. Counsel for the defence can and must stand by. Yet her duties under the Code in respect of the law are clear, namely to

> ... ensure that the Court is fully informed of all relevant decisions and legislative provisions of which he is aware whether the effect is favourable or unfavourable towards the contention for which he argues.[22]

Hence, a strict interpretation of the rules would invite laziness in respect of the search for legal materials and dishonesty by omission in respect the facts.

As Pannick observes more judiciously, there is a fine line between where the duty to one's client ends and a barrister's obligations to society and the court begin.[23] Thankfully, counsel is not bound to degrade herself for the purpose of winning her client's case. Yet people who are attracted to the Bar are fire-fighters – competitive, with an interest in winning. How far should they go? For example, is the use of a sensible tactic in a civil claim – having your expert in court – intimidatory in a criminal context? Or, does her presence merely serve to restrain an otherwise over-enthusiastic prosecution expert? Is it playing by the rules or to the rules?

Those criminologists interested in the sociology of law would argue that this question invites no easy answer. For abuse of the rules and use of the rules cannot be neatly separated. The distinction between tax avoidance and tax evasion, is, in the hands of lawyers, one which constantly shifts as the lawyers' advice enables clients to work to the very limits of the law and exploit *lacunae* in it.[24] Equally, McBarnet's earlier (1981) and seminal work detailed how the rhetoric of the law is routinely subverted, with the resulting dissonance being able to exist *'and be resolved* within the law itself; the ideology can also be managed within the law's own institutional structure'.[25] To McBarnet:

Law in this form is like a Russian doll. You begin with the
rhetoric and a single apparently definite condition, which
on closer inspection turns out to contain another less clear
condition which in turn opens up to reveal more ifs and buts
and vagueness, reducing so often to the unpredictability of 'it
all depends on the circumstances' – which criteria we use in
your case depends on your case.[26]

The law, therefore, is a tool not only to be used, but one which
also – according to the standpoint from which it is observed –
invites 'abuse'.

For example, the good closing speech is designed to lay
bare whatever doubts there may have been in the jury's mind
on hearing the evidence. But, some would argue, it may be
used to sow seeds of doubt – how certain is certain? For
how long must you remain sure beyond a reasonable doubt?
Today, tomorrow, forever? The criminological literature on
dangerousness illustrates well how future uncertainty can
undermine and pollute current confidence. The client will reap
the rewards – whatever they are – of the jury's deliberations.
So, how does the barrister live with the very real possibility that
his or her efforts have not merely presented the case for the
client, but contributed to the construction of doubt and thereby
led to the acquittal of the guilty?

The answer to this question may lie with the source of the
propulsion of many criminal practitioners' efforts. I would argue
that barristers may justify their tenacity partly by reason of the
relative barbarity of the punishment that follows conviction. If
criminologists and barristers agree about one thing, it is the sheer
futility of imprisonment. Barristers may lag somewhat behind,
retaining a belief in the incapacitative impact of prison, but they
certainly do not conceive of it as an instrument of 'change for the
better'. Moreover, the question, 'who is the victim?' when posed
at court provides an interesting lesson in side-lining. The goal
posts are all too readily moved. The client may well be guilty
and found so, yet one's sympathies can extend to him when,
after the event and in the artificial light of most court-rooms,
the convicted offender is sentenced to imprisonment. Together

with him, and it is usually him, are sentences of separation for those who have supported the defendant through the trial and who have most to lose – wives, girlfriends, mothers and children. Imprisonment is a wretched form of punishment. And for those involved in death penalty appeals to the Privy Council from other jurisdictions ,the motivation is even more apparent.[27] Any ground and every ground must be pursued. But, is the avoidance of an overly punitive response a sufficient basis for the acquittal of the guilty? Better it be that ten guilty men go free than one innocent be convicted. What if the odds were altered to 100 to one or 1,000 to one? It is these issues with which barristers may struggle; it is in that arena in which they certainly must perform. Sitting on the touchline, hurling abuse, is a legitimate role for the researcher.

Responsibility

Researchers are expected to draw conclusions from their enquiries and make recommendations. A cynic might argue that such recommendations can be made in the knowledge that they are unlikely to be taken up by policy-makers for reasons, for example, of cost or changed conditions since the research was conducted. The time lag for most empirical enquiries makes this inevitable. Researchers are not encouraged or even expected to push for their policy recommendations – merely to explain their basis. To advocate too strongly might imply an axe to grind or some erosion of their independence. Researchers tend not to be agitators. When not adopted, researchers can sit back and say, 'they (the policy-makers) are the ones without the imagination or courage to respond'. Indeed, we can make our recommendations with reference to the general and not the particular. Hence, Block et al. advocated the abolition of committals on the grounds that they provide a false focus for Crown Prosecutors and do little or nothing to prevent inherently weak cases passing through to the Crown Court.[28] We recommended substitution by a simple transfer to the Crown Court, with the option for the defence to argue before a judge that there is no case to answer. This is not a conclusion from which, as a criminologist, I would now seek to dissociate myself. But, in the potential role of counsel for the defence the issue is less clear. Abolition would mean no more paper committals, but no more s.6(1) committals – where live evidence can be tested – either. Functioning in the real world of conviction and acquittal leads some members of the Bar to argue that s.6(1) committals have an important function. Although as a means of intimidating reluctant witnesses, or as fishing expeditions, or as rehearsals of lines of cross-examination they may have few proponents, more honourable motives do exist. As one of my pupil supervisors amply illustrated, the opportunity to understand an expert's testimony may only come once. If it comes only at trial and the prosecution have the monopoly on both experts and the requisite forensic evidence then injustice may result in the individual case where counsel cannot properly test the evidence without first understanding it in the dry-run an s.6(1) committal provides. Of course, this may be an argument for changing the nature of forensic evidence, for having more pre-trial hearings or whatever.[29] But in some limited cases s.6(1) committals do perform a vital function. And the barrister's horizon is invariably this case, this battle and not the war. Indeed, the war may never come.[30]

At the Bar, the notion of responsibility and the duty to one's client can mean to say everything possible on behalf of the client – to leave no stone unturned. Full pursuit does not mean getting at some quintessential truth; in bald terms it means doing your best for the client; more baldly still – winning. There is a clear interest in outcome – the end justifies the means. Indeed, the process of discovery – going laboriously through the means – can itself lead to defences not previously uncovered, unimagined mitigation or unexpected outcomes. For example, where a client insists on pleading not guilty where he has no credible defence (or one not credible to his counsel) he nonetheless has a right to put the prosecution to proof of his guilt. Where a client makes this decision on grounds *not* divulged to counsel, for example, he believes because he has actively assisted the police that they will favour him in their evidence, and it is only during the course of the trial that this misconception emerges, the client may still benefit from some charges failing where civilian witnesses, as not infrequently occurs, do not come up to proof. Thus, where counsel proceed on the basis of imperfect knowledge, as they necessarily frequently do, working to the boundaries of the law may prove beneficial to the client where prosecutorial error or incompetence favours them. Moreover, although the practice of plea bargaining continues to be frowned upon, prosecutors' conflicting duties facilitate bargaining. The duty to charge to the highest the evidence will allow is inconsistent with the notion that prosecutors should not 'throw the book' at an accused. The consequence is that over-loaded indictments invite bargaining by both sides. An accused is likely to be convicted of something – be it not the principal charge – and defence counsel can help to reconcile the accused to an outcome. In this scenario there are no losers.

Finally, advocates are not ciphers. Where clients are legally aided, the barrister owes a three-way duty; to court, to client and to the Legal Aid Board. Where a case looks hopeless, the barrister is obliged to inform the Legal Aid Board and support may well be withdrawn. Where an offer of settlement is made, the barrister must inform the Board whether the offer is acceptable. In these circumstances barristers do have a safety-net that enables them to make judgments about clients and conceivably to work actively to demonstrate that their cause is unworthy. Counsel can exploit both the presence of legal aid in resisting a settlement, its absence when creating pressure for a settlement to be accepted[31] and its overriding interest when hopeless causes are being pursued by clients unwilling to give up the struggle.

Conclusions

The *modus operandi* of barristers and researchers contrasts sharply in three areas. The context in which their work occurs, the consequences that stem from it, and the extent to which they can either associate with or distance themselves from that work.

First, context. Practice means doing urgent battle, juggling with issues that may or may not come good and in the knowledge that however much preparation can be undertaken, things may well go wrong due to the unpredictability of witnesses and their testimony. Clients themselves are not immune from this and are 'imperfect' in many other ways, including behaving with 'limited rationality'. It is not easy, and barristers do get things wrong, particularly when called upon at a moment's notice. The errors and omissions create a sense of imperfection in the barrister's daily life, but have many parallels with other practitioners. As Irving and Dunnighan have detailed amongst CID officers, the roots of imperfection are to be found primarily in cock-up rather than conspiracy.[32]

The researcher, however, strives for perfection. Pilot work, fine-tuning and endless re-writing are their stock-in-trade. Every word, every assertion has to be justified; footnotes, citations and self-citations abound. Moreover, once in print, all may be subject to challenge from sources then unimaginable for a period without end.

In the world of justice, actors behave sometimes from frustration and irritation – the fine-defaulter who is sent to prison by a busy lay bench in a mood of exasperation goes there inappropriately. Even the bench may feel less than happy, but the moment passes; and the appeal, particularly with an unrepresented defendant, may never threaten, let alone arise. Yet, the ever-present illusion of being able to have 'one more bite at the cherry', through the possibility of appeal, can make tolerable the immediate impact of the barrister's losses.

But the most penetrating distinction lies in their identification with their work. Even those barristers who pursue the most noble causes ultimately do it for others and to others. Researchers are defensive about their work because it *is* a reflection of them – even if only at a particular moment in time. Claiming that their ideas have moved on since the work was conducted has the perfect smoke-screen in the publication time-lag. Academics may equally jealously guard their ideas and seek public recognition by having their names attached to, or divorced from, every thought. Hence, the 'minority report' or the 'note of dissent'. Barristers can be exonerated because they are only doing – admittedly to the best of their ability – the bidding of others. Much of their work is negotiated in private and buffered by the role of the solicitor. Polite criticism has been formalized and barristers are, by and large, supportive. Even court performances, about which barristers are rightly sensitive given the need to impress client and solicitor, may be one step removed from those waiting to pounce on the barrister's failings or make a judgment about further instructions. It would be cynical to suggest that performance is the barrister's only yardstick; but its importance, in contrast with the content or cause, should not be underestimated. Researchers, however, are called upon in the most adversarial of settings – the academic conference – to defend their ideas, their methodology and their conclusions, in short, themselves. It is little wonder that a gulf persists.

Notes

1   See, for example, J. Plotnikoff and R. Woolfson, *Information and advice for prisoners about grounds of appeal*, Royal Commission on Criminal Justice, Research Study no. 18 (HMSO, 1993), citing widespread ignorance about the mechanisms of the criminal appeal system; and C. Hedderman and D. Moxon, *Magistrates' Court or Crown Court? Mode of trial decisions and sentencing*, Home Office Research Study no. 125 (HMSO, 1992), on the role of misconceptions in the decision about mode of trial. See also D. McBarnet, *Conviction. Law the State and the Construction of Justice* (London, Macmillan, 1981), on the limits of law: 'the rhetoric of criminal justice is routinely subverted in practice by its practitioners, whether through the non-legal motivation of the policeman on the beat or through the reasoning powers of High Court judges.'

2   See A. Ashworth, E. Genders, G. Mansfield, J. Peay and E. Player, *Sentencing in the Crown Court*, Occasional Paper no. 10, Centre for Criminological Research (University of Oxford, 1984). The then Lord Chief Justice, Lord Lane, barred further research on Crown Court Sentencing, whilst the then Lord Chancellor, Lord Hailsham, slated the work – both on the basis that research could tell the judiciary nothing useful; their response to reports of misconceived practices was that 'if it was happening, it shouldn't be'.

3 Royal Commission on Criminal Justice, *Report* (HMSO, 1993). The report's thrust is one of efficiency, whereas academics had anticipated a focus on means of addressing the injustices revealed by the miscarriage cases of the 1980s. Suggestions that submissions made to and research conducted for the Commission were 'subjective' (see, for example, Royal Commission on Criminal Justice, *Report* (HMSO, 1993), chapter 5, para. 39), and thereby, valueless, were neither welcome nor justifiable where research methodology went unacknowledged by the Commission.

4 I am grateful to my pupil supervisors, Nicholas Paul and Stephen Irwin of Doughty Street Chambers, and David Watkinson of 2 Garden Court, for sharing their cases, their observations and their time with me.

5 D. Pannick, *Advocates* (Oxford University Press, 1992), p. 2.

6 E. H. Sutherland and D. R. Cressey, *Criminology* (10th ed.), (J. B. Lippincott Company, USA, 1978).

7 Ironically, the early part of my nascent career as a barrister has been spent with much hand-holding of anxious clients at court, reassuring those who have been in fear – sometimes even of physical assault – and in providing explanations of procedures and outcomes.

8 J. Shapland, *Between Conviction and Sentence: The Process of Mitigation* (London, Routledge and Kegan Paul, 1981), p. 120.

9 D. Pannick, op. cit., p. 132.

10 Ibid., p. 10.

11 C. Corbett and F. Simon, 'Decisions to break or adhere to the rules of the road, viewed from the rational choice perspective', *British Journal of Criminology*, no. 32 (1992), pp. 537–49.

12 D. Pannick, op. cit., p. 23.

13 R. Hood, *Race and Sentencing* (Oxford, Clarendon Press, 1993).

14 B. Block, C. Corbett, and J. Peay, *Ordered and Directed Acquittals in the Crown Court*, Research Study no. 15, Royal Commission on Criminal Justice (HMSO, 1993).

15 M. Maguire, F. Pinter and C. Collis, 'Dangerousness and the tariff: the decision-making process in the release from life sentence', *British Journal of Criminology* no. 24 (1984), pp. 250–68.

16 J. Peay, *Tribunals on Trial: A Study of Decision-Making under the Mental Health Act 1983* (Oxford, Clarendon Press, 1989).

17 *Bar News*, no. 56 (1993), p. 1.

18 M. McConville, A. Saunders and R. Levy, *The Case for the Prosecution* (London, Routledge, 1991).

19 See, for example, the attrition rate reported in S. Grace, C. Lloyd and L. Smith, *Rape: from recording to conviction*, Home Office, Research and Planning Unit Paper No. 71 (HMSO, 1992). Of 335

alleged cases of rape or attempted rape, there were 89 convictions for rape and 47 convictions for lesser offences.

20 General Council of the Bar, *Code of Conduct of the Bar of England and Wales* (Bedford Row, London, 1991), para. 202.

21 Pannick, op. cit., p. 107.

22 *Code of Conduct of the Bar*, para. 610 (c).

23 Pannick, op. cit., p. 7.

24 D. McBarnet, 'It's not what you do but the way that you do it: tax evasion, tax avoidance and the boundaries of deviance' in D. Downes (ed.), *Unravelling Criminal Justice* (London, Macmillan, 1992).

25 D. McBarnet, *Conviction. Law, the State and the Construction of Justice*, p. 168.

26 Ibid., p. 161.

27 Doughty Street Chambers, where I undertook my first six months of pupillage, regularly represented such clients.

28 B. Block et al., op. cit., p. 76. Ironically, Watkins LJ in *R v. Attaway and Cunningham* (unreported judicial review 1993) noted that even if there were no evidence on which the magistrates could have reached their decision to commit, he would have been very reluctant to quash the exercise of their discretionary decision.

29 See, in particular, the recommendations of the Royal Commission on Criminal Justice, *Report* (1993), chapter 9.

30 Only a small proportion of cases in both the civil and criminal systems turn into contested trials; invariably, pleas and settlements result. Where a trial does take place the brief may well go to another barrister – being switched at the last minute due to a listing procedure outside the control of individual barristers.

31 H. Genn, *Hard Bargaining: Out of Court Settlement in Personal Injury Actions* (Oxford University Press, 1988).

32 B. Irving and C. Dunninghan, *Human Factors in the Quality Control of CID Investigations*, Royal Commission on Criminal Justice Research Study no. 21 (HMSO, 1993).

II

RECOLLECTIONS AND REMINISCENCES

1

VICTOR BAILEY

I have the strong feeling that most people remember vividly the first time they met Jane Morgan. For me it was mid-way through 1979 in the city of Oxford. A year before, I had become a research fellow of Worcester College, thanks to the support of Sir Leon Radzinowicz and Dr Roger Hood, eminent criminologists both; of John Croft, head of the Home Office Research Unit; and of Lord Asa Briggs, Provost of Worcester. After a year working solo on a history of modern criminal policy, I was given the go-ahead to hire a research assistant. I coaxed the selfless College 'servant' and historian, Harry Pitt, and the gifted yet unpretentious criminal lawyer, Andrew Ashworth, into helping interview the shortlisted candidates.

We held court in Harry's imposing first-floor rooms, over-looking the front quad and gardens, watched languidly by Harry's dog (which was by tacit agreement a 'cat', since College still debarred resident Fellows from owning anything other than felines). Jane's file described a woman of considerable accomplishment, efficiency and drive. The arrival of two children had delayed neither completion of the Ph.D. nor co-authorship (with historian husband, Ken) of what would become *Portrait of a Progressive: the Political Career of Christopher, Viscount Addison* (1980). Ken was, we knew, among other things, a Welshman of average height. Hence, our surprise when in strode a figure who towered over all of us. We met a woman, moreover, of undoubted vivacity, with eyes that transfixed us. She embraced an executive briefcase, whose clasps had been broken (I later learnt) by a typically impulsive attempt to make it hold a cabbage from Oxford market. Her interview went swimmingly, the only sign of unease being a slightly nervous laugh. It could have been much worse. The night before she had commandeered Ken for service as mock interviewer, but on entering the lounge, she had invariably collapsed into paroxysms of laughter.

We had no hesitation in offering her the job; and I had not one moment's regret about our decision during the two years that Jane and I worked together. Two years of trekking to Kew, not to sample the botanical delights of the famous Gardens, but to enter the mausoleum that is the Public Record Office and decipher the administrative remains of Home Office and Prison Commission. On the road, in those two years, we discussed every topic under the sun; few knew me better than Jane, and I knew few better. Through Jane, I learned an inordinate amount about Wales, women and Oxford University. To Jane, I owed the introduction to Ivon Asquith at Oxford University Press, which would eventually publish my *Delinquency and Citizenship*. In Jane, I marvelled at the prodigious energy that was required of protective wife, devoted mother, historian, teacher, and rider. (No colleague since has invited me to help with the purchase of a horse box!) It was as if Jane knew that time was short and she would have to work fast.

Nor did I once regret asking the Senior Common Room to grant Jane dining rights on High Table. Or perhaps I did, at first, for I recall feeling miffed when French historian and revered raconteur, Richard Cobb, who had already dismissed me as a 'red' for having joined a rearguard action to defeat his motion to cancel the SCR's subscription to the *New Statesman*, ecstatically welcomed Jane's SCR membership. I moodily put his behaviour down to his known Welsh sympathies. It is not particularly easy to be a part-time member of an SCR, although Worcester was a remarkably friendly place, but Jane was a natural. I can see her now, interrogating Fellows and guests, mildly flirtatious, a shameless name-dropper, unassuming about her own achievements, yet never intimidated by anyone more enamoured of their reputation. I knew then that I loved her to death; and even beyond.

When my own career took me first to Hull University, and then to Kansas, I saw Jane but rarely. I managed to keep track of her academic successes, however. We would occasionally correspond; letters from my good friend, Roger Hood, filled in other gaps; and in recent years, my senior colleague, J. P. Kenyon, would return with news of Jane from British Academy parties. I was especially delighted to see the publication of *Conflict and Order* (1987), since I had suggested, when her job with me came to a close, that she might examine policing in inter-war Britain. This became, in her creative hands, a splendid study of the police and labour disputes between 1900 and 1939, a study which has rightly informed the vigorous public debate of recent years concerning the principles and practices of policing. Jane Morgan remained in the criminological field until the end, a field to which, I take great pride in saying, I first introduced her.

2

SUE BALSOM

My abiding memory of Jane is of a tall, glamorous first-year history student in 1968, returning along Aberystwyth's promenade to Alexandra Hall for supper. I was definitely in awe of Jane's seemingly effortless composure and a self-discipline that kept her in the Old College Library until six most evenings. Our conversations, though, would be less than earnest – a gossipy mix of student news, the latest antics of library and academic staff, and other girls' boyfriends.

Even then, Jane displayed a remarkable social awareness and a talent for making friends easily from completely different walks of life and of all ages. She simply knew everyone and liked good company. Above all she was interested in people and this was reflected in her academic interests, both in social history and the welfare issues she chose to champion. Although she often denied it, Jane always struck me as someone who knew where she was going. She was composed and able to gauge priorities; she had career objectives such as her Ph.D., research and publications, yet she could be disarmingly frank and very amusing about the conflicting pressures on modern women. She was totally committed to her children, enjoyed a passionate marriage and proved herself time and again in her academic work, as well as fulfilling public service appointments.

Jane's great personal good fortune was her marriage to Kenneth and their children, David and Katherine, and she wished as much for others. She successfully introduced several couples and delighted in the birth of friends' children. In my case, children came quite late and although we had stayed in touch for over fifteen years, when my first daughter finally arrived, the shared experience of motherhood immensely enriched my friendship with Jane.

Anyone attending parties at Long Hanborough would be introduced to leading figures from academia, journalism and politics as well as neighbours, riding friends and old college chums. This eclectic group reflected Jane's easy, egalitarian approach and her tremendous loyalty to friends for whom all the privileges of Oxford and the Morgans' wide political circle would be brought to bear if help or advice was required. Her willingness to encourage and ease access to decision-makers was part of Jane's natural grace and success as a hostess. She firmly believed that to get things done one should go to the top and 'top' people were fortunately as captivated by Jane's charm as anyone else.

Jane's return to Aberystwyth in 1989 as the Principal's wife came at a difficult time in respect of her work on a Home Office research project and the children's education. At the same time she was determined to support her husband's go-ahead plans for the University. Staff morale and prospects for higher education had experienced difficulties and their arrival at the helm gave Aberystywth a much needed fillip. A change of mood was soon apparent in the official residence, Plas Penglais. The rather gloomy, austere house was soon transformed and became the focus of receptions and lively dinner parties. But before refurbishing the formal rooms, Jane's first priority was to establish intimate family quarters more suited to the needs of teenage children and their friends.

Charged with the difficult task of managing a family and two homes, being Aberystwyth's First Lady and writing up her research, Jane set herself a punishing schedule. Few were aware of the miles covered each week as she endeavoured to carry out her additional duties as an Oxfordshire magistrate, her contribution to Victim Support and work for the Welsh Arts Council. Meanwhile, there were seminars and talks on her joint book with Dr Lucia Zedner, *Child Victims*, and at one stage Jane even managed to fit in a spell teaching at the University College in Bangor.

Many saw only that sparkling smile, those intelligent, kind eyes and Jane's supreme elegance, and these are rightly what we should remember. I am privileged to see Jane's mother, Jessica Keeler, from time to time and to continue to see much of Jane in David and Katherine who display her determination, strength of character and personal qualities so magnificently. In them I see her beauty, her courtesy and love of life. However, I cannot forget the brave fight against such a cruel disease that so quickly robbed us of Jane's presence. I regret the cowardice that prevented my admitting she would die so soon and I recall her great fortitude and dignity as she slipped away. To this day I simply cannot believe she is not dashing about the country somewhere, and I store up news and conversations we might have enjoyed.

My thoughts and feelings were echoed by Lady Jay on the day of Jane's funeral service, when she said, 'We have lost a really good girl-friend, haven't we? A real "mate".'

Indeed we had.

3

HENRY PHELPS BROWN

Many of those whose lives were enriched by their friendship with Jane Morgan will long continue to cherish the indelible impression that she made upon them at their first meeting. Here, unmistakably, the thought in glad recognition would arise, was a Gainsborough portrait living and moving in our midst – the pure, clear colour of cheek and eye, the graceful poise and the lithe carriage, conferred immediately a distinction that might well have set her on an eminence at some remove. But she herself had no thought of that: her approach was friendly, open, simple and direct, natural and unaffected. Hence her genius for friendship, and her outstanding gifts as a hostess, whether on formal or domestic occasions. These were only part of her amazingly untiring activities, maintained without derogation to her role as wife and mother. There was a time when on one day in each week she would drive through the mountains to conduct a course in the Department of Law at Bangor; then drive back, and make her way across country into Bedfordshire to spend the evening conducting interviews as part of the fieldwork for her study of child victims; thence returning to reach home by midnight. Days at home she might begin by rising at dawn to muck out the stable of her noble Orlando; the late evening would see her completing her stint on the word-processor. Yet always she had time for her friends, to whom she would convey something of her own zest for living. She got so much done, because of her remarkable capacity to work rapidly, and of the courage with which, as author, no less than as rider, she took her fences. Once, when advised that a script on which she had worked long and hard should be recast and rewritten throughout – a verdict that would have proved devastating to many a scholar already weary of the too familiar material – she set herself to the task, and worked long hours to bring it to an acclaimed conclusion. There was within her a free-flowing fount of vigour. It is hard now, for us who remain, to believe that the source of such vitality can have been stopped so suddenly for ever. We must think it possible that some belated wayfarer in the Oxfordshire lanes, looking up at the sound of approaching hoof-beats, may yet discern through the mists of evening, the figure of Jane, sitting high and supple on Orlando, homeward bound.

4

DICK HOBBS

My introduction to Oxford University bore little relation to dreaming spires and scholarship. Rather, it was damp guest-houses off the Woodstock Road; persuading the guardians of the Bodleian's treasures that my intent was scholarly and not villainy; negotiating the in-bred meanness of the University's inmates; and supporting a growing family on a contract researcher's salary. Then I met Jane Morgan and her concerns were 'Did I have anywhere to live?', 'Was my family OK?' and 'What had I written?' in that precise order. Despite by the mid-1980s being very much part of the Oxford scene, Jane fully understood the terror that the misty city with its veiled and heavily coded rituals could invoke in new arrivals. While I was left to stew in my own ever-ripening juice by colleagues fully marinated in the mire of the academy, Jane Morgan attempted to deconstruct for myself and my family the tedious strangeness of Oxford life.

Her first concern was housing, 'Where are you going to live? These are the best areas, meantime come and stay in our attic.' She spent hours explaining how Oxford worked, and even longer reading my Ph.D. dissertation, of which both she and her husband Kenneth were most complimentary. To this day, I am most grateful to these two historians for the gentle manner in which they pointed out such minor historical errors as placing the Huguenots in the wrong century and muddling the reigns of Elizabeth I and Henry VIII.

There were few teaching posts available in 1985 and Jane worked around the clock as a researcher on 'Crime UK' before commencing her study of victims. All of this was carried out at the Centre for Criminological Research, and Jane's office was the place where people could go for a good gripe. Visiting scholars from both home and overseas were also beneficiaries of Jane Morgan's wit and wisdom, and dinner at the Morgans' home was the highlight of many a sabbatical. Apart from the research, numerous publications, informal counselling sessions and entertaining, Jane also brought up two children in an atmosphere of gentle integrity. Katherine and David were regular visitors to the CCR, for Jane neither hid her children away nor wore them like a badge. They were part of her life rather than the burdensome appendage that so many middle-class offspring mutate into. The school pick-ups and extra-mural clubs were often followed by a long drive to interview victims of crime or to a Victim Support meeting. All this while successfully negotiating with that most soul-destroying governmental tool, the Home Office.

Jane had little in common with civil servants, nor with senior police officers; their cold indifference and rigidity found no favour with Jane Morgan, who would usually return from Queen Anne's Gate or some provincial police headquarters resentful and ever so slightly manic. These institutions, upon which she relied for both funding and access, were male-dominated and Jane had to deal with various forms of sexism not only from grey men in suits and Her Majesty's Constabulary, but also from academics who misread Jane's vivacious elegance for a lightweight intellect.

This was an enormous mistake and Jane explained on several occasions how male academics in particular often associated female dowdiness with intellectual depth, and unhygienic masculinity with enigmatic genius. The fact that Jane dressed smartly and resembled neither an ageing hippy nor a power-dressing businesswoman from hell confused some people, as did her ambition to own a Paul Costelloe jacket and her admission that in times of stress she would confide in her hairdresser.

This therapy obviously worked, for Jane was rarely without an infectious grin. Grants could run out, colleagues impose impossible deadlines and some malady infect the children, but Jane Morgan would come up grinning with a series of self-effacing stories that would brighten up all but the most bovine individual's day.

Not everybody appreciated someone who could publish in the fields of history and criminology, bring up two happy, healthy children, lead an active social life, enjoy a successful marriage to another eminent academic and still not take herself seriously. Further, Jane Morgan had the audacity to be a Labour Party supporter while failing to live in abject poverty. Yet Jane's detractors were few and her popularity unmatched by any other academic of my acquaintance. Jane also had an aggressive streak and although she did not relish conflict she could, if backed into a corner, be effectively combative. Jane's explanation for this referred to her upbringing in Wrexham, a background she neither advertised nor denied but of which she was fiercely proud.

When Kenneth was appointed Principal at Aberystwyth, Jane's immediate joy was quickly tempered by her understandable concern at uprooting her family. Typically, she coped with this traumatic time with her familiar mixture of sensitivity and good humour, and a year later I found myself being counselled by Jane as I and my family also contemplated a traumatic guilt-ridden move northward.

Apart from a couple of all too brief meetings I lost contact with Jane, and found out about her death by accident. Like most defaulting debtors, I always intended to pay Jane Morgan back, but somehow didn't quite make it.

It may be crass to say that I miss her more now than when she was alive but it's a fact. I don't know if Jane ever got her Paul Costelloe jacket, but I bet her hairdresser misses her. My enduring memory of Jane Morgan relates to one wet spring morning in Oxford. Jane's contract was almost finished and she had no idea if further funding was forthcoming. I was slumped over a table in the general office whining that I had only a year left on my contract. Jane kicked my backside and as I sharply stood up, painfully surprised at such an unexpected assault upon my dignity, she rapped me on the head with a wad of papers and trilled 'cheer up' before descending the stairs to her office laughing raucously.

Jane Morgan was a class act, sorely missed.

5

ROGER HOOD

I remember vividly the first time I met Jane Morgan because she expressed so fervently her desire to become a criminologist. That was towards the end of 1979. She had been introduced to me by Victor Bailey, my former pupil and colleague, who had recruited her to be his assistant on a historical study of juvenile delinquency in the twentieth century. Victor was delighted to find someone so well qualified as Jane. She had had a sound grounding in history and sociology at Aberystwyth, had completed a successful Ph.D. dissertation at Leicester on political history, and had just published, in collaboration with her husband, the distinguished historian Kenneth O. Morgan, a political biography of the progressive politician, Viscount Addison. I had therefore not been expecting to meet someone with such a passionate interest in criminology. How, she asked me, could she get into the field – bearing in mind, of course, that she had two young children and a husband and was not free to go elsewhere to pursue further study?

Such a direct line of questioning was, I soon learned, typical of her. Not that she was pushy. Indeed she was, perhaps, over-modest about her considerable abilities and achievements. Rather, it was indicative of her determination: a determination to work in a field of study which she conceived to be not only inherently fascinating but also of central importance to the well-being of citizens and the maintenance of a just society. What better, I said, than to begin by working alongside a social historian and criminologist, particularly on a subject which was bound to bring her into contact with all the core problems of criminology: the definition of crime and delinquency in historical perspective; the problems of assessing the state and trends of crime; the various theories, both lay and academic, which have purported to account for crime; and the social and political ideas and interests which shape reactions to crime and give practical expression to them in legislation and penal practice. So it was that her work with Victor Bailey paved the way for her induction into the subject.

It was in 1982 that I invited Jane to become a research associate of the Centre for Criminological Research. She had just been awarded a research fellowship of the British Academy to undertake a study of the role of the police in labour disputes in England and Wales between 1900 and 1939. This work was based on a thorough study of public records and on many local archives up and down the country. It was not only further testimony to her determination and thoroughness of work but revealed also her remarkable gift for establishing good personal relations. Her vivacity, charm, and abundant energy no doubt helped. But perhaps more important was her ability to communicate her genuine interest in people and what they did. Hitherto-closed sources of material were opened to her and interviews were readily granted. Indeed, she soon proved to be especially adept at this art form.

When she came to the end of this work, and while preparing her highly acclaimed book, *Conflict and Order: the Police and Labour Disputes in England and Wales, 1900–1939* (which was published by Oxford University Press in 1987), Jane began her work on contemporary criminological issues. Soon, she said – her eye still upon her ultimate goal – she would be able confidently to call herself a real criminologist. Her opportunity came when the centre was approached by Anthony Harrison, who was anxious to find an academic home for his new enterprise Crime UK and someone gifted to work on it full-time. Jane, ever-eager, took up the challenge. The resulting successful publications in 1986 and 1988 dealt with the costs of crime and, in particular, with the problems of estimating the resources that both the public and private sector were contributing to crime prevention and law enforcement. But much as this interested Jane, it was in many ways too removed from immediate problems as they affected those whose lives were blighted by crime.

Recognizing her real and sincere interest in the impact of crime on people, I had asked her to join me in the University–Prison discussion group which I, or another member of the centre, held every week at Oxford Prison. The purpose of this group was to bring together criminology students and prisoners over four hour-and-a-half meetings to discuss the way in which the inmates viewed their experiences of crime and punishment. It does not take much imagination to perceive the sensitive nature of these meetings. Jane's warmth of personality and fearless direct approach were the ideal combination for getting the best out of such a situation. Sympathetic as she was to the plight of the prisoners, she had no hesitation in asking them to account for their apparent lack of consideration for their victims and the families who were suffering without them. Courage, skill, and above all, warmth of personality were the qualities which enabled her to raise such a delicate question in the prison setting without sounding either sanctimonious or patronizing.

Around this time I had heard that Jane had been appointed a Justice of the Peace. It was an aspect of her public life which she never let intrude upon her academic work, partly I suspect out of modesty, for she was held in high regard by her colleagues. Jane also played a valuable role within the British Society of Criminology and went on to become a most successful editor of the Society's *Newsletter*.

She had also developed an intense interest in the plight of victims of crime through her contact with the pioneering work done at the centre by her colleagues Joanna Shapland, Mike Maguire and Claire Corbett. Jane resolved to work in this field herself. Towards the end of 1986 she submitted to the Home Office a proposal for a study of the effects of crime on children which immediately received a favourable response. Soon afterwards the national charity, Victim Support, suggested that the research might incorporate an evaluation of the pioneering work being done in this area by the Bedfordshire Victim Support Scheme. The novelty of this project created considerable publicity and excited high expectations when it was announced. The scope of the fieldwork that Jane had planned was formidable for a project to be carried out by two people: interviews with all the agencies who dealt with children in both Oxford and Bedfordshire; analysis of police and Victim Support records; and interviews with child victims and their parents. It required enormous dedication, involving as it did long and unsocial hours of work. Yet again the activist, Jane trained as a Victim Support volunteer and was to remain dedicated to this work.

Jane was the first to recognize that she was having to learn 'on the hoof' techniques of research and, more difficult, how to analyse and present a complex mass of material drawn from several sources. She was at first helped by Joyce Plotnikoff and then by Lucia Zedner who became the joint author of *Children as Victims of Crime*, published by OUP in March 1992. Jane and Lucia remained exceptionally close friends and were working together on yet more articles when Jane was so tragically struck down. Their book was justly regarded as the first to focus upon, and to discuss rationally and sympathetically, the role that could be played by the police, prosecution, courts, and the statutory and voluntary social agencies in alleviating the effects of crime on the young. It could only have been done by someone with that blend of political practicality and academic zeal which Jane so markedly possessed. It firmly established her in criminology: where she always wanted to be.

My final thoughts are of Jane as friend and colleague. Not just to me but to all with whom she worked. Her *joie de vivre*, ebullient spirits, sense of humour, and genuine concern for people, enlivened by a sharp perception of their strengths and weaknesses, had a binding effect on the life of the Oxford Centre, to which she remained closely attached as a research associate after her move to Wales. She was much loved and is sorely missed.

6

HELEN MUIR

My last memory of Jane was when she was briefly at the Royal Marsden Hospital in Surrey, having her first bout of treatment, a few weeks before she died. She wasn't in her own room, which was stuffed with flowers and cards, but I found her sitting in a big room with Ken, and some other visitors, attached to a drip.

She was in her nightdress, gone suddenly thin. She was obviously feeling weak and ill because her eyes kept closing, but she stood up, managing the cumbersome apparatus, and came to greet me, starting to move a chair forward and giving the same welcome she might have given at one of her parties. Her spirit was not crushed. She never stopped being *dashing*.

I knew Jane for about seventeen years, from the times we used to meet at guest night dinners at Queen's College, Oxford, (when Ken was a Fellow), and I counted her as a very special friend. Although I live in London and she lived in Oxford, then Wales, we met when we could and had long chats on the telephone in between. We had our shared interest in writing books and literary events and gossip. Jane was very funny. She always had lovely stories to tell and she listened. You could almost hear her listening. She got the point instantly, as the good friend must. She was most perceptive about people and, as far as friends were concerned, she never forgot for a minute about the things that mattered to them in their lives.

That's what I miss now: her vitality, the amusement and her support. She was always thinking of ways to help. A part of her, Jane said herself, remained at heart the hard-working little girl from Wrexham, who grew up without her father, with the Welsh dedication to education. But she had another side; she was somebody with a natural amused awareness of how the world worked. She made things happen, she managed so much and she made it all look easy.

One thing she stage-managed in her earliest days was her first meeting with Ken. She used to see him regularly, sitting in the library and longed for him to speak to her. Week after week she went, knowing he would be there and waited hopefully for him to look up and notice her.

When the day came that he did invite her for a cup of coffee, she unfortunately had another engagement to which she didn't admit. They had coffee, then Ken offered to escort her home and, reluctant to break the spell, Jane simply got on the tube with him. Racked with anxiety about the passing time and her missed appointment, she travelled many miles in the wrong direction. However, that unrelaxing journey paid off because quite shortly afterwards, reader, she married him.

Jane loved her family dearly. She would have been proud of her children, David and Katherine, who stood bravely beside their father after the funeral and greeted every member of that crowded congregation as they came out of church. It must have been a great ordeal for two teenagers who had had to cope with the loss of their mother so suddenly.

So much has happened since the early days of her married life, but now it seems such a little while ago that Jane was musing in bewilderment on the mysteriously lax ways of the daily help. 'She doesn't move the furniture when she's vacuuming', she said, 'I don't know how to tell her to do it because I've never given orders to anyone before.' In the end she wrote a note, 'Please hoover under the furniture.' The woman wrote back giving notice.

After the move to Aberystwyth when Ken was appointed Principal, Jane, a marvellously serene hostess by that time, was naturally hesitant to tamper with existing methods of running Plas Penglais. She was very conscious initially that the spotlight was upon them locally and there would be comment on any new decisions. She did, however, notice that before dinner only one drink was offered to guests and she asked if a larger measure

could be provided for a second one, if desired. As this new rule
was implemented, she was somewhat taken aback to overhear
the shocked voice of one of the Welsh waitresses declaring:
'They're drinking like fishes.'

But Jane seemed to settle easily into the life in Aberystwyth.
After all, she was coming to a familiar place where Ken's mother
lived and she had been at university herself. She continued to
work for the Centre for Criminological Research at Oxford but
grew steadily more and more involved with local projects.

Jane told me once that what she wanted most in the world
was power. The power she already had she used well. When
she died at forty-two, most people might have thought that
with her marriage, her children, her horses, her criminology
work, her academic law lecturing and her books, plus being
a magistrate and a member of the Welsh Arts Council, she had
done enough for anyone. I suspect that Jane would have felt she
was only just beginning.

As I was preparing to write this piece, a spiritualist told me
she could see a woman in her forties with dark hair and dark
eyes who had died suddenly of cancer. I asked what she was
saying. 'I don't think she's saying anything', she said, 'She seems
to be listening. I think she's listening for the right words.'

I can imagine her standing with that little half-smile. I hope
these are the right words. The only words really are to say how
sad it is without her. I was frightfully fond of Jane.

7

J. P. WOODSTOCK

If this piece were nothing more than a simple valedictory, it
could never adequately describe the delicious sense of fun
that Jane brought to our sometimes depressing work on the
Woodstock Magistrates' Bench.

Jane's humour and deductive powers were revealed within
seconds of first meeting. Our current bench chairman recalls

the supreme irony of lay persons interviewing an eminent criminologist as a prospective magistrate. The selection panel was probably as apprehensive as Jane herself. Would she fit in? Would she be too clever? Would she know more than the clerk? They need not have worried. They had no hesitation in recommending Jane for appointment to join the other diverse characters of the Woodstock Bench since the lively personality and sensible approach shone through, even in response to general questions such as, 'Why do you want to be a magistrate?', 'Have you discussed this with your husband?' and 'Tell us about prison classes at Oxford'.

Our Justice's Clerk recalls that his concerns on his own appointment were about how he would relate to members of the Woodstock Bench, since he probably expected our tiny historic coterie to be extremely aristocratic and dim-witted. Although there were indeed some members of the nobility, he concedes the latter part of this initial premise was entirely wrong, as on meeting us he quickly, or diplomatically, decided we were intelligent and conscientious: but Jane was the 'pearl'.

People whose sole experience of the law is by way of television dramas may be unaware that along with our training, newly appointed magistrates are also expected to observe a couple of proceedings before being permitted to adjudicate. A few days after appointment, I was therefore given the apparently simple instruction to introduce myself to my new colleagues and then join the public area of whichever of the two courts had the more interesting case load. Since we occupy what must be one of the most unsuitable buildings for a courthouse in the country (a grand, bechandeliered and ancient Town Hall somewhat inadequate for modern judicial needs), persons unfamiliar with the layout frequently appear unannounced in the room where we discuss matters before formal business starts. What felt like a sea of heads turned towards me, all but one apparently convinced that this mystified novice JP, sorely in need of a 70-per-cent-proof confidence booster, was yet another miscreant who had blundered amongst them, looking for somewhere to wait for their case to be called. However, a chuckling female voice immediately broke the silent tension with a gleeful, 'It's nice to know I'm no longer the new girl. I'm Jane. Pleased to meet you.' She had instantly assessed the situation and within seconds put the magistracy's rawest recruit at ease by whimsically explaining how a year earlier she had faced identical problems before triumphing over the unhelpful facilities of our historic edifice.

A magistrate, particularly one on a bench as small as Woodstock, does not deal with criminal matters only. Licensing, family, juvenile, committee, training and other court obligations rapidly fill a diary. With her hectic schedule, Jane rightly resented any time-wasting. It was at bench meetings where her experience shone through. She always fought her corner with considerable determination and polite charm, saying very little, but when she did speak she invariably curtailed further debate, convincing waverers and silencing opposition with a dozen well-chosen words. This was most evident in the months leading to the introduction of the Children and Criminal Justice Acts. Our clerk remembers with fondness the many interesting and lively discussions he had with her at that time about aspects of law and society, adding, 'We were both involved in writing books and articles, although I was very much in the fourth division compared to Jane's premier league.'

In that quotation lies the clue to our admiration. It was not just the concepts she put forward, the principles she held or expertise brought to our varied roles that we so admired. Jane certainly marshalled her reasoning with awesome clarity and employed this logic to strike at the very heart of an issue. However, most impressive was that on those few occasions when we assembled our own counter-arguments with a matching degree of acumen, she was sufficiently open-minded to come across to the opposing point of view. Nevertheless, while happy to discuss or guide us on a wide range of issues, woe betide those who stuck to their guns on the basis of mere opinion and not fact. As luck would have it, she once sat with a chairman of very long standing on a day when the court list held a wide variety of unusual cases rather than the normal tedious catalogue of motoring offences; the third member was a very raw but strong-willed magistrate. The venerable individual spent an infuriating morning sandwiched between the younger generation. The worthy did not actually wish to ship out the guilty to Botany Bay, nor would he have returned the Bloody Tower to its original purpose. Nevertheless, after he had been repeatedly out-voted two to one and long before the lunch-time recess, Jane was having difficulty suppressing her laughter since the senior appeared to be gazing longingly at the stocks not 50 metres from the Town Hall and trying to recall if any statute gave them the power to place amused and unmanageable junior magistrates within its ancient timbers.

In due course, Jane completed her own chairmanship training (the instruction of magistrates on how to conduct a court), and was anxious to get on with the job and start leading sessions for herself. She admitted enjoying the feeling of being in control, and was therefore irritated at the same people regularly taking the centre seat. A haunting memory of our bench chairman is the phone call she received when Jane was already ill. In a bright and very happy voice Jane remarked how brilliantly she was getting on, had had time to think, to put things in perspective and apologized for being such a nuisance about taking the chair. Even at the end she was still displaying that unique combination of driving leadership, merriment and sensitivity.

Levity is all very well, but magistrates obviously need to present a persona of seriousness and solemnity when on view. Jane therefore delighted in those moments when away from the public gaze and free to make a private, apposite and frequently entertaining remark. Thanks to her, one local solicitor will for ever be known to some of us as the man 'unsuitable for any work other than delaying court proceedings'. Similarly, the claim of a motorist who tried proving mathematically that the speed of 102 m.p.h., measured electronically by the police, was really in the low 80s was dismissed as follows: 'Our horse could have seen the flaw in that piece of arithmetic.' Yet very few of Jane's observations were critical. She praised another solicitor with the words, 'I learned much about the successful espousal of apparently lost causes this afternoon.' Similarly, she personally commended a junior clerk, who had explained a tricky point of law in the retiring room, that her pithiness would be much appreciated in the university's law department.

Finally, perhaps most telling about Jane's attitude as a magistrate, was the occasion when three of us were faced with a particularly knotty case concerning a lady in early middle age. As we considered whether a very lenient sentence was appropriate, Jane murmured with a wry smile, 'If my upbringing had been as wretched as hers, and then I'd been let down so badly, I'd probably be facing similar serious charges.' Thereafter we were in no doubt that compassion was the correct decision.

Innumerable further recollections from Jane's colleagues illustrating her humour, understanding, dedication and enthusiasm for public service could be cited. Most would end with something similar to our bench chairman's, 'What an immense loss the magistracy has suffered', or the clerk's, 'I will greatly miss her.' For himself the writer will merely conclude that unlike Jane, he does not believe in a heaven. However, he now has no doubt there is an afterlife. There must be, since she lives on, still guiding those who sat with her as each in turn recalls her myriad astute observations.

Jane Morgan – A Bibliography

1. Books

(with Kenneth Morgan) *Portrait of a Progressive: the Political Career of Christopher, Viscount Addison* (Clarendon Press, Oxford, 1980, 326 pp.).

Conflict and Order: the Police and Labour Disputes in England and Wales, 1900–1939 (Clarendon Press, Oxford, 1987, 305 pp.).

(with Lucia Zedner) *Child Victims: Crime, Impact and Criminal Justice* (Clarendon Press, Oxford, 1992, 203 pp.).

2. Articles

'Denbighshire's *annus mirabilis*: the Borough and County Elections of 1868', *Welsh History Review* VII, No. 1 (June 1974), 63–87.

'Getting better use of police resources', *Crime UK* 1986 (Policy Journals, London, 1987).

(with Anthony Harrison) 'Efficiency and off-loading in the Criminal Justice System', ibid., 1988.

'Children as victims', in M. Maguire and J. Pointing (eds.), *Victims of Crime: A New Deal* (Oxford University Press, 1988), pp. 74–82.

(with Joyce Plotnikoff) 'Children as victims of crime: procedure in court', in John Spencer et al. (eds.), *Children's Evidence in Legal Proceedings: an International Perspective* (Cambridge, 1990), pp. 189–92.

(with Lucia Zedner) 'When the victim is a child: some issues for the Criminal Justice System', *The Magistrate*, April 1992.

(with John Williams) 'Supporting child witnesses in criminal proceedings', *The Magistrate*, September 1992.

(with Lucia Zedner), 'Child victims in the Criminal Justice System', in D. P. Farrington and S. Walklate (eds.), *Offenders and Victims*, British Criminology Conference, 1991, Selected Papers, Vol. 1 (London, 1992), pp. 238–60.

(with John Williams) 'Child witnesses and the legal process', *The Journal of Social Welfare and Family Law*, 1992, No. 6, pp. 484–96.

(with Lucia Zedner) 'The Victim's Charter: a new deal for child victims?', *The Howard Journal of Criminal Justice*, Vol. 31, No. 4 (November 1992), pp. 294–307.

(with John Williams) 'A role for a support person for child witnesses in criminal proceedings', *British Journal of Social Work* (1993), 23, 113–21.

(with Lucia Zedner) 'Researching child victims. Some methodological difficulties', *International Review of Victimology* Vol. 2 (1993), pp. 295–308.

(with Frans Winkel and K. S. Williams) 'Protection and Compensation for Victims of Crime' in P. Fennel, C. Harding, N. Jorg and A. H. J. Swart (eds.), *The Europeanization of Criminal Justice* (Oxford University Press, 1994 forthcoming), chapter 16.

3. Reports

'A Breviate of Parliamentary Papers relating to Wales, 1868–1964' (Board of Celtic Studies, Cardiff, 1975).

(with Lucia Zedner) 'Children as Victims of Crime: a Report to the Home Office', 1990, 148 pp.

A Report to the National Association of Victim Support Schemes 1990: 'An Evaluation of a Demonstration Project on Child Victims in Bedfordshire', 20 pp.

(with John Williams) A Report to Dyfed Family Health Services Authority 1991: 'A Consumer Survey of General Medical Services', 30 pp.

4. Conference Papers

(with Joyce Plotnikoff) Paper on 'The child witness and the court', International Conference on Children's Evidence in Legal Proceedings, Cambridge, June 1989.

Workshop conducted with Joyce Plotnikoff on 'Children as forgotten victims' at the British Criminology Conference, Bristol, July 1989.

Paper on 'Children – the forgotten victims of crime', The British Criminology Conference, 1990.

Paper on 'Victim Support and child victims', Annual Conference of the National Association of Victim Support Schemes, June 1990.

Paper on 'Child victims in the Criminal Justice System', The British Criminology Conference, July 1991.

5. Editorship

British Society of Criminology *Newsletter*.

Index

Subscribers to this volume

The following have associated themselves with the publication of this volume through subscription:

Paul Addison, Edinburgh
A. Ashworth, London
Ivon Asquith, Oxford
Caroline Benn, London
Lord Blake, Norwich
Vernon Bogdanor, Oxford
A. Keith Bottomley, Hull
D. George Boyce, Swansea
Susan Brayshaw, Newtown
Stephen Brooke, Halifax, Nova Scotia
Hugo and Mary Rose Brunner, Oxford
Natasha Burchardt, Oxford
Marilyn Butler, Oxford
Lord Callaghan of Cardiff KG
Quentin and Ann Campbell, Oxford
Muriel E. Chamberlain, Swansea
John Cable and Susan Charles, Aberystwyth
Owen Chadwick, Cambridge
Margaret and Brian Clarkson, Swansea
Lord Cledwyn of Penrhos CH
Ann Clwyd and Owen Roberts, London
Jill and Jon Cohen, Oxford
Allison Coleman, Aberystwyth
Lord Crickhowell
Alun G. Davies, Beaconsfield
Aneurin and Betty Davies, Swansea
Carys a Rees Davies, Aberystwyth
G. Henton Davies, Saundersfoot

Jayne and Derek Davies, Newtown
Lord and Lady Davies, Llandinam
Megan ac Alun Creunant Davies, Aberystwyth
Graham Day, Llanfairfechan
R. E. and R. P. Dobash, Cardiff
Martin Eckley, Harlech
J. W. England, Harlech
Gareth Wyn Evans, Cardiff
J. Wynford and Mrs Evans, Cardiff
D. Ellis Evans, Oxford
Vivian and Glenys Evans, Senghenydd
Sheila Forster and Jonathan Jones, London
Ann Ffrancon a Geraint H. Jenkins, Aberystwyth
Hywel and Mair Francis, Neath
Irene and Michael Freeden, Oxford
Pat Gale, Richmond, North Yorkshire
Loraine R. Gelsthorpe, Cambridge
E. H. H. Green, Oxford
W. P. Griffith, Bangor
John D. Griffiths, London
Ralph A. Griffiths, Swansea
John Grigg, London
R. Geraint Gruffydd, Aberystwyth
John and Mary Habakkuk, Oxford
Neil and Deanna Harding, Swansea
B. H. Harrison, Oxford
Cameron Hazlehurst, Zillmere, Australia
Peter Hennessy, London
John and Bridget Herries, Witney
Roger Hood, Centre for Criminological Research, Oxford
Lord Emlyn Hooson, Llanidloes
Janet Howarth, Oxford
Daniel W. and Mrs Howe, Oxford
David W. Howell, Swansea
Elinor and John Hughes, Aberystwyth
Hugh R. Hughes, Aberporth
R. A. and S. R. Humphrey, Milfield, Northumberland
Bruce Hunter, London

Richard W. Ireland, Llanilar
Douglas and Mary Jay, Oxford
Aled Jones, Aberystwyth
Alun Gwynedd Jones, Bethesda
Emyr and Megan Wyn Jones, Pwllheli
Gwerfyl Pierce Jones, Aberystwyth
R. Brinley and Stephanie Jones, Porthyrhyd, Llanwrda
Daniel and Maureen Gruffydd Jones, Aberystwyth
Gareth Elwyn and Katherine Jones, Pennard, Gower
J. Gwynfor Jones, Cardiff
Sir Richard Lloyd Jones, Cardiff
R. Merfyn Jones, Bangor
Sharon Louise Jowitt, London
Morton Keller, Cambridge, Massachusetts
Alan and Alwen Kemp, Cardiff
Laurence Koffman, Aberystwyth
Elaine Koss, New York
Helen Krarup, Cambridge
John E. Law, Swansea
D. C. Mansel Lewis, Llanelli
Roy Light, Bristol
Countess of Lisburne
Dilys Wynne Lloyd, Cardiff
Lewis W. Lloyd, Harlech
Peter and Olive Madgwick, Oxford
Mike Maguire, Cardiff
Geoffrey Marshall, Oxford
John Martin, Manchester
Lisbeth Mason, Oxford
Sue and Colin Matthew, Oxford
G. W. McKay, Oxford
Ross McKibbin, Oxford
Fergus and Susanna Millar, Oxford
Judge Lord Elystan Morgan, Bow Street
Jane a Derec Llwyd Morgan, Aberystwyth
Kenneth O. Morgan, Aberystwyth
Delyth Morris, Bangor
Stewart and Joy Neal, Machynlleth

Tim Newburn, London
Sir David Nicholas, London
George Noakes, Carmarthen
Arwel Ellis Owen, Taffs Well
Brian Owen, Llanidloes
Huw and Mary Owen, Aberystwyth
I. Dale Owen, Penarth
Alastair Parker, Oxford
Stephen Parrott, London
Cyril Parry, Bangor
James T. Patterson, Providence, Rhode Island
Ken Pease, Stockport
Henry Pelling, Cambridge
W. J. Phillips, Carmarthen
René Pillorget, Paris
Ben Pimlott and Jean Seaton, London
Joyce Plotnikoff, Hitchin
Chris Powell, Bangor
J. O. Prestwich, Oxford
D. J. Prosser, Dorking
Sir Leon Radzinowicz, Cambridge
Peter Raynor, Swansea
David Harding Rees, Rome
Nan and Graham Rees, Aberystwyth
Keith and Janet Robbins, Lampeter
G. Roberts, Bangor
Hywel a Jennifer Roberts, Bow Street
W. J. C. Roberts, Aberystwyth
Arthur and Dilwen Roderick, Lampeter
Sir Melvyn Rosser, Swansea
J. S. Rowett, Oxford
Ann a Roy Saer, Caerdydd
Joanna Shapland, Sheffield
A. J. S. Shelton, Fontainebleau
The Lady Silkin of Dulwich
Sally Simon, Richmond, Surrey
M. A. Simpson, Swansea
Beverley and Llinos Smith, Aberystwyth

Dai Smith, Barry Island, South Glamorgan
E. B. Smith, Cardiff
Garfield Smith, Llansteffan
Robert W. Steel, Swansea
Elan Closs Stephens, Aberystwyth
Gillian Stern, London
Leslie and Freda Stone, London
D. Arwyn Thomas, Cefneithin
Geoffrey P. Thomas, Oxford
John R. Thomas, Wrexham
Sir Keith Thomas, Oxford
Nan and Barrie Thomas, Aberystwyth
Christopher Turner, Cowbridge
John Vincent, Bristol
David and Margaret Walker, Swansea
Philip Waller, Oxford
John and Frances Walsh, Oxford
Philip Wareing, Aberystwyth
A. M. C. Weale, Aberhonddu
Baroness White of Rhymney
Raymond White, Llangunnor
H. G. Williams, Bangor
J. Gwynn Williams, Bangor
John Williams, Aberystwyth
John and Ina Tudno Williams, Aberystwyth
Katherine S. Williams, Aberystwyth
Moelwyn I. Williams, Aberystwyth
Stephen Williams, Oxford
Chris Wrigley, Nottingham
J. C. W. Wylie, Cardiff
Ken and Brenda Young, Gerrards Cross
Zaleha and Arshad, Selangor, Malaysia
Zawiyah Baba, Kuala Lumpur, Malaysia

Aberystwyth Old Students' Association
Arnold Lodge Secure Unit Staff Library, Leicester
C. E. Bazell, Magistrates' Clerk and Staff, Banbury
Bedfordshire Police

Bodleian Law Library, Oxford
The Brotherton Library, University of Leeds
Cleveland Constabulary
Coleg Harlech Library
Community University of the Valleys, Banwen
Community Rights Unit, London Borough of Southwark
Department of Extra-Mural Studies, University College of
    Wales, Aberystwyth
Goldsmiths College Library, London
Institute of Criminology, University of Cambridge
Llyfrgell Hugh Owen Library, University of Wales, Aberystwyth
Salisbury Library, University of Wales College of Cardiff
South Wales Miners' Library, Swansea
Staff Development Unit, North-east London Probation Service
Trinity College, Carmarthen
Victim Support, National Office, London